Study
Smart Junior

The Princeton Review

Study
Smart Junior

Studying Your Way to Stardom

by Chris Kensler

Random House, Inc.
New York
www.randomhouse.com/princetonreview

Princeton Review Publishing, L.L.C.
2315 Broadway
New York, NY 10024
E-mail: comments@review.com

ISBN 0-679-77539-0

Editor: Gretchen Feder
Production Editor: Julieanna Lambert
Designer: Scott Harris
Illustrator: Dorothy Marczak
Production Coordinator: Scott Harris

9   8   7   6   5   4   3

To Bob Block and Henry Kensler and Warren Tamms

ACKNOWLEDGMENTS

The author thanks Heather so much. And he also thanks everyone who worked on this book: Gretchen Feder, Julieanna Lambert, Laurie Barnett, Greta Englert, Dorothy Marczak, Neil McMahon, and Scott Harris.

CONTENTS

Introduction for Kids

Hey, you! Yeah, you. Listen up. Learning and studying aren't the same thing.

Learning is natural. It's what humans do best. Your ability to learn tons of stuff is what separates you from frogs, shrubbery, and concrete.

Need examples? Okay. You learned that the toaster oven is hot by burning your hand. You learned to tie your shoes by doing it over and over again. You learned how to make your parents go nuts by cutting your own hair and listening to loud music . . . or was that me?

School, on the other hand, is a place where learning doesn't always come naturally. Where learning comes from studying. You don't want to make your parents go nuts by doing poorly in school, because in reality you know you are only hurting yourself.

Study—what a terrible word. Let's look at its definition, provided by the folks at American Heritage Dictionaries.

study (*v.*) **1.** To apply one's mind purposefully to the acquisition of knowledge or understanding of a subject. **2.** To read carefully. **3.** To memorize. **4.** To take a course at school. **5.** To inquire into; investigate. **6.** To examine closely; scrutinize. **7.** To give careful thought to; contemplate.

That didn't help much. I still don't like the word. It sounds scary, solemn. "To scrutinize." "To read carefully." "To apply one's mind purposefully." Jeez. What do these things mean?

I like to approach studying a different way. Do you agree?

In life, you learn about things in a thousand different ways. In school, you learn one way—by studying. Studying involves three—and only three—simple steps:

1. Getting it.

2. Remembering it.

3. Writing it down later.

This book, *Study Smart Junior*, focuses on these three simple studying steps. Four fun-loving characters, whose first names all start with the letter "B" for some reason, are here to lead you through a series of adventures and, yes, *exercises* (I hate that word, too) that will help you to learn how to:

1. Get it.

2. Remember it.

3. Write it down later.

We will explain the mysteries of how to study so you can get good grades and stop agonizing about school. So, let's get on with it already.

Chris Kensler

New York City, 1999

INTRODUCTION FOR PARENTS

This book, like all books, will mostly benefit the student who learns best by reading—a visual learner. If your child is an auditory learner, one who learns best by listening, it will help if you work through the book with her, reading aloud and discussing the various exercises and scenarios together.

This book offers interesting ideas to make studying more fun. For example, we encourage students to get the phone numbers of a couple of schoolmates in each class for emergency study contacts and to create "study posters" (see page 124). These are posters that students make to help them learn, visualize, and remember school assignments. Everything in this book— along with the story that links all the exercises—is designed to get your child *involved* in learning. All students learn best when they are involved in *active* learning, which means *learning by doing*. That means reading with a pencil (see chapter 5), making calendars and schedules for school and free time (see chapter 3), and "actively relaxing" before a test or quiz (see chapter 7).

Your child can read *Study Smart Junior* and complete the exercises on her own, but if you take a role in your kid's education, the improvement will be even more dramatic. Read along with us so that we can all study our way to stardom together!

How This Book Works

Study Smart Junior is the story of how Babette learns to study more effectively so that she can realize her dream of becoming a fashion designer for the aging pop star Felton Jack. She and her close friends—including a talking cat—go on a bunch of adventures through which Babette learns how to make a school schedule, take useful notes, and study for a test, all to become a better overall student.

You can learn along with Babette and her friends by following their sometimes funny, sometimes harrowing journeys, and by completing a variety of exercises and multiple-choice quizzes. Important study skills that Babette picks up on her journey are highlighted as a series of study tips. You can become entranced by the incredibly fascinating tale, do all the exercises and quizzes, and then go back and just reread the tips in each chapter to review everything you and Babette were supposed to learn. So, there's

1. A story.

2. Exercises and quizzes.

3. Study tips.

These three elements make up *Study Smart Junior* and offer the easiest, most fun, most complete way for you to learn and remember good study habits.

THE CAST OF CHARACTERS

Babette

Babette is a native of Paris, France. Coming from Paris, she has a great flair for fashion. A bit preoccupied with boys and being popular, she's always been an okay student, but not a great one.

Barnaby

Barnaby is a supergenius, so he's never had trouble doing well in school. He's done so well, in fact, that he's now a teacher at Babette's middle school, even though he is the same age as Babette.

Bridget

Bridget goes to the same school as Babette and Barnaby and is currently the European tour manager for the pop band Grandson. She does well in school because she's very organized.

Beauregard

Beauregard is a cat that can talk. He hails from South Carolina but is keeping Babette company in New York these days. A bit of a ladies' cat, Beauregard is never lonely. His favorite food is Bumblebee tuna in oil.

Brenda

Brenda is a calico cat. Beauregard is a little sweet on her. She doesn't have much to say but "meow."

Felton Jack

Felton Jack is an aging pop singer whose personal fashion designer, Kiki Krayola, has died. Without a good clothing designer, Felton, who is quite unattractive, is doomed.

Grandson

Grandson is a very popular pop band. The band has three members, all brothers, Ihop (guitar), Thackeray (drums), and Sailor (vocals, tambourine).

Chapter 1
The Dream

SATURDAY

It was a warm Saturday in late August. Babette lay by the lake in New York City's Central Park, thinking about the new school year, scheduled to start on Monday.

"I'll wear my new black Calvin Klein jeans," she thought, "and my new black Ralph Lauren tank top and my new black Ray-Ban sunglasses and my new black Doc Marten boots, and I will look good.

"Shane Fusselman will finally see me for the incredibly stylish girl that I am, and he will ask me to go steady, and I will say 'Shane, I love you, and I will be your steady girl.'

"Then, Bobby Deakes will finally see me for the incredibly stylish girl that I am, and he will ask to carry my books, and I will say to him 'Bobby, I carry my own books, I am an independent girl, but I love you, and I will break Shane Fusselman's heart and be yours forever.' Shane will be crushed, but thankful for the minutes we had together.

"In third-period science Trish Matthews and Carly Poptart will see me for the incredibly stylish girl that I am and ask me to be their friend, and I will say, 'You are the most popular girls in school, and I have always wanted to be as popular as you, so, yes, I will be your friend.'"

And so Babette imagined her first day of school and the following days—the boys chasing after her, the popular girls begging her to be their friend, and the stylish clothes she would wear, and then she drifted off to sleep. Lying by the pool on that hot August day, the back-to-school issue of *YM* at her side, Babette, slathered in suntan lotion and full of hope for the coming school year, dreamed the dream that would change her life.

BABETTE'S LIFE-CHANGING DREAM

Above the lake (now filled with rose petals) across Central Park (now strewn with thousands of bouquets) stood the entertainer loved by millions, Mr. Felton Jack, barefoot, wearing a plum silk Kiki Krayola five-button suit, a yellow silk Kiki Krayola shirt, and orange, oval glasses designed by—you guessed it—Kiki Krayola.

"Wonderful!" said Babette, rising from her lounge chair, plastic straps sticking to her sweaty back.

"Felton!" she called. "Mr. Jack! You look marvelous! Bravo!"

He looked her way, but before Felton could reply, a strong wind descended—as if from heaven—and blew across the petal-filled lake, raising a red, fragrant cloud that collected all the petals from the bouquets strewn across the field until the air was a kaleidoscope of color.

The colors—pink, tangerine, plum, ecru—were magical. Babette snatched at the air, brought the flowers to her face and breathed in deep. She looked to Mr. Jack with tears of joy in her eyes.

Mr. Jack was gone.

"Mr. Jack!" she yelled. "Mr. Jack!"

Mr. Jack had disappeared. Babette waded through the petal storm, calling all the time, "Mr. Jack! Mr. Jack!" Finally, the magical storm subsided, and there, head down, stood the entertainer loved by millions—Mr. Felton Jack—wearing only a huge pair of heart-covered boxer shorts.

"Noooooooooooooooooo!" screamed Babette. "Noooooooooooooooo!"

"Yes," he said. "This is me stripped of my finery. Not pretty, I know, but true. I am washed up! I have no talent! Can anyone help me?"

Babette screamed again, horrified by the boxer shorts-clad image of her idol.

"Please child, I beg you! Now that my close friend Kiki Krayola has gone to that great runway in the sky, nobody can figure out how to make my homely, blubbery figure look stylish. My career is in serious peril! I have tried wearing overalls but they make me look like an overweight farm wife. I have tried baggy pants like the kids wear these days, but there are no pants so baggy that they look hip on me!"

Felton Jack sniffled into his hand. "It's just my luck. Right after I'm knighted by Queen Elizabeth, on everyone's guest list, invited to so many, many teas and lunches with more sandwiches than you can imagine—salami, turkey, roast beef with mayonnaise. Sandwiches!"

"Control yourself, Mr. Jack," advised Babette.

"Sorry. But I'm upset! I can't go out in public because the only designer who ever made me look pretty, Mr. Kiki Krayola, is dead! Oh, the irony!"

"That's not really irony," corrected Babette. "Irony is like when Alanis Morrisette sang in her great song, 'isn't it ironic when . . .'"

"But you get my drift!" interrupted Felton. "Don't you?"

Babette did. "I will help you," she said, looking deep into his worried eyes. "I will devote my life to designing clothes especially for you, Felton."

"Thank you, my little crocodile rock," he gasped, holding her hand. "Thank you, my little Marilyn Monroe."

"My name is Babette."

"Okay," he said. "How can I repay you?"

Babette thought for a moment. "You know the song you wrote in the late seventies? 'Little Queenie'?" she asked.

"Yes," he replied.

"Could you rewrite it as 'Little Babette,' the way you rewrote 'Candle in the Breeze' for your good, tragic friend Princess Pi? 'Little Queenie' has always been one of my favorites."

"Consider it done!" squealed Felton Jack. "Now go! Learn the fashion craft! Clothe me, Seymour! Clothe me!"

"My name is Babette."

"Yes," he said. "Little Babette. Now run along, and when you return with designs that will make me presentable to polite, civilized society, I will sing you your personal ballad." And, with that, Felton Jack turned and walked away across the field of bouquets, his whiter-than-white body glistening in the sun.

BABETTE SETS A GOAL

Babette woke with a start. A large, black cat rubbed its back on the bottom of her lounge chair, back and forth, purring loudly and strongly. The water had no petals on it. The bouquets were gone from her field of dreams.

"Oh, Beauregard!" she exclaimed to the cat, picking him up. "I know what I'm going to do with my life!"

Beauregard looked at her with annoyance in his eyes. He did not like being picked up.

"I'm not going to waste my time on insignificant things like what to wear to school. I'm not going to wonder if Shane Fusselman likes me or not, and I'm not going to worry about being the most popular girl in class. Instead, I am going to get good grades so I can be a fashion designer! But so much more than that, I'm going to get good grades so I can be Felton Jack's fashion designer! He is loved by millions, you know."

Beauregard gave her a weird look. "How are you going to become Felton Jack's fashion designer?" he asked, for he was a special cat that could talk.

"By getting into Fashion High School," explained Babette. "That's where Ralph Lauren went to high school, it's where Calvin Klein went to high school, it's where Donna Karan went to high school. All the top designers in New York started there!"

Biggest Mongo Tip of All Time!: Set a Long-Range Goal for Your Life

It's good to have a goal when you're in school. Things get hectic, classes get hard, you wonder how facts about the Revolutionary War could possibly help you later in life. Having a goal keeps you listening, and it keeps you working. And we don't mean a goal like "I want to get straight Bs" or "I want to study twice as much as I did last year." We're talking about goals like "I want to travel to China before I'm twenty," and "I want to win the Nobel Peace Prize," and "I want to be Felton Jack's fashion designer."

Having a long-range goal gives you a reason to do all the little things you have to do to get good grades, like dissecting frogs, learning long division, and studying. Your long-range goals can change; they will probably change a hundred times, but always have one in your mind to keep you motivated.

My long-range goal on this date, _____, is to
_____.

Date:_____
New Long-Range Goal:_____.

Date:_____
New Long-Range Goal:_____.

Date:_____
New Long-Range Goal:_____.

"And how are you going to get into Fashion High?" asked Beauregard. "That's one of the hardest high schools to get into."

"By studying and getting good grades in middle school, *mon chat*," replied Babette.

"*Mon chat*? What does that mean?" asked Beauregard.

"It means 'my cat' in French."

"Oh. Anyway, how are you going to get good grades?" continued Beauregard. "So far, you haven't piled up too many As or Bs, and you've been studying pretty hard."

"That's true," said Babette. "I cannot study much harder. What should I do? I am doomed!"

"Relax, dear Babette," offered the cat, using her leg as a back-scratcher. "You are not doomed. I have an idea."

"What is it? What is it?"

"Instead of studying harder, why not try studying better?"

"What does that mean, *mon chat*?" asked Babette, removing his shed hair from her calf.

"What does *mon chat* mean again?" asked Beauregard.

"I am sorry. It means 'my cat' in French."

"Okay. Fine," said Beauregard.

"And what does 'study better' mean again?" she asked.

"Well, Babette, you study plenty long, so you can't really study much longer. You try hard, so you can't really try much harder. Therefore, I suggest you do a few different things to improve your grades."

"I'm down," said Babette.

"I'm sorry you're still upset," Beauregard said, trying to console her.

"No, 'I'm down' means 'I'm all for it.' I want to learn to study better." explained Babette. "It is your American slang, no?"

"You're asking the wrong cat," replied Beauregard. "I do not use human slang terms. Slang makes me want to cough up hairballs. Anyway, with school just a few days away, I know that the first thing we have to do is get you your school supplies."

"Groovy baby, yeah!" exclaimed Babette.

Beauregard coughed up a hairball.

QUICK SUMMARY OF CHAPTER 1

★ Babette is looking forward to the first day of school because she likes Shane Fusselman and Bobby Deakes and she wants to be in the popular group of girls this year.

★ Babette has a dream where the singer Felton Jack pleads with her to be his personal fashion designer.

★ Babette wakes and decides to devote her life to clothing the aging pop star. This is her long-range goal. You should have one, too.

★ The problem is, she doesn't get very good grades, and to get into Fashion High—where all the great designers went to high school—she must do really well in middle school.

★ A talking cat, Beauregard, suggests that studying *better* instead of *harder* may help her get higher grades in school. She is excited and wants to know more.

Chapter 2
Getting the Right Supplies

SUNDAY AT SCHOOL SUPPLY-O-RAMA

Beauregard knew that Babette needed to stock up on school supplies, so he took her to New York City's most fashionable school-supply store.

School Supply-O-Rama was jammed with back-to-school shoppers. Babette and Beauregard made their way through aisle after aisle of boys and girls looking at backpacks, moms yelling, and dads in tears. Every shelf was filled with paper, pens, pencils, notebooks—you know the scene.

"Can you get off my hem?" Beauregard growled at Babette. He was disguised as a grumpy old granny because the store does not allow cats.

"Sorry," said Babette. "There is *soooo* much school stuff here. Where do I start?"

"Where do you usually start?"

"In sportswear."

Smart Shopper Tip:
Be Prepared from Day One

You know you're off to a bad start when you show up on the first day of school unprepared. You have to write all your notes in one notebook, stuff all the handouts you get in one folder, borrow a pencil from your neighbor, and all that kind of stuff. Before the school year starts, you need to get the basic materials you'll need for classes—pens, pencils, a three-ring binder, a calendar, computer disks, and spiral notebooks.

Once school starts, each teacher will probably ask you to get a few other things, like a protractor for math class and a daily journal for English class. Just make sure you have the basics for the first week of school, and buy the specialty items as you need them.

"You mean you never buy school supplies before school starts?"

"Oh sure, I usually get the latest, coolest Trapper Keeper and some pens and pencils, and maybe some paper."

"That's a good start, Babette. But you must get more." From a fold in his granny gown, Beauregard pulled a piece of paper.

"Each year of grade school my mother, dear Beatrice, rest her soul, sent me and my seven brothers and sisters, dressed as old women, to the school-supply store with this list."

School Supplies

Make a ☑ by each school supply

General

- ❏ Backpack
- ❏ 10 pencils with erasers
- ❏ 10 pens (blue or black)
- ❏ 1 Hi-Lighter
- ❏ 1 big eraser
- ❏ 1 pencil sharpener
- ❏ 1 three-ring binder
- ❏ 200 sheets of lined paper
- ❏ 200 sheets of typing or computer paper
- ❏ 10 computer disks
- ❏ 1 dry-erase board that fits on your locker door
- ❏ 1 wall calendar
- ❏ A stapler and staples
- ❏ Index cards
- ❏ Paper clips
- ❏ Post-it Notes

For each class

- ❏ 1 one-subject spiral notebook
- ❏ 1 one-subject folder with pockets

"That is a lot of stuff," said Babette, looking longingly down the aisle to where girls and boys were trying on gym shoes. "But if you say I need it, then I need it. I refuse to blow my chances at good grades by not being properly prepared with notebooks and pens and whatever else."

"Good for you," said Beauregard, and they stocked up on everything from his dear mother's school supplies list. They stood in line for an hour, paid for it all, then fought their way out of School Supply-O-Rama.

That night, Babette had a restless sleep. Dreams of popularity, Shane Fusselman, Bobby Deakes, and Felton Jack competed with one another for Babette's attention.

Quick Summary of Chapter 2

★ Beauregard and Babette went to School Supply-O-Rama to stock up on school supplies.

★ Babette usually started the school year with just a few things. Beauregard told her she needed to start out prepared for every class.

★ Beauregard gave Babette a list of school supplies that his mother had made for him when he was a kitten going to school.

★ Get the all the stuff you need for school before school starts. It's the first step to being prepared for class every day.

Chapter 3
Making Your Own Schedule

MONDAY

Babette arrived at Mellman Middle School for the first day of school in her new black Calvin Klein jeans and her new black Ralph Lauren tank top and her new black Ray-Ban sunglasses and her new black Doc Marten boots and her backpack full of school supplies. She looked very nice and prepared. She went to her assigned locker and dumped everything in it.

Tip for the Sloppy:
Keep Your Locker Organized

If you have a locker at school, you know how out-of-hand it can get. Before you know it, it's just a pile of crumpled paper and old banana peels. To stop this from happening, try keeping your locker organized. Put the books for your morning classes on top and the books for your afternoon classes on the bottom.

To make sure you bring the right books home each night, get an erasable marker board. Write your classes on it and check off after each class that requires you to bring your books home to study.

Math	☑
English	☑
Social Studies	☐
Science	☐

The next day, erase the checks and start over.

Shane Fusselman noticed her in first-period English.

"Hey there, Babette," said Shane, leaning over from his desk, running his fingers through his perfect hair. He smiled the smile that last year melted her lonely heart. "How was your summer vacation?"

"Oh fine, Shane, and yours?" replied Babette nervously.

"Terrible," said Shane.

"I am sorry, why?" asked Babette.

"Because you were not a part of it."

Babette blushed.

"Babette?" asked Shane, running his fingers through his hair. "Dear Babette?"

"Yes?" replied Babette.

"Will you be my steady girl?"

Just as Shane Fusselman asked her the question she'd dreamed all summer of him asking, their English teacher, Mr. Blister, handed out the assignments for the week and a list of topics they would cover in the first semester.

"Here, class, are your assignments for the week and a list of topics we will cover this semester," he said. "Now, class, I expect assignments in on time, neatly written on paper that is free of food and beverage stains."

Babette looked at the assignments. Babette looked at Shane. Shane ran his fingers through his hair, then blew her a kiss. Mr. Blister burped.

"Excuse me," said Mr. Blister.

Babette looked back at the assignments, took a deep breath, and answered Shane.

"Shane, you are a special friend, and I'll always remember this day, this very moment, as one of the happiest, most special moments of my life. But I cannot go steady with you. I am committed to another man."

"Who?" demanded Shane, full of jealousy.

Tip for the Mega-Popular: Make School Numero Uno

To do well in school, you have to make it your first priority. Don't worry, *you will still have fun* (especially if you stay organized, which we'll discuss more later). Just make sure school comes first, and everything else comes second.

"A singer."

"Which singer?"

"That I can't tell you. He's from England, so you'll probably never meet him. But I do care for you, Shane, and I always will."

With that she leaned over to his desk, kissed Shane's perfect forehead, tucked her English assignment lists in her red English folder, and class began. Mr. Blister began his lecture on John Steinbeck's classic novel *Of Mice and Men*.

"John Steinbeck was a great writer," he began. "Great writers write great books. This is a great book."

Within minutes, half the class was looking out the window, dreaming of a summer vacation that had ended too soon, but not Babette.

In second-period math, the story was pretty much the same. Babette got her math textbook, a list of topics that would be covered in the semester, and a list of assignments for the week. She tucked them in her math folder, and gently told Bobby Deakes that he would have to find another girl.

In third-period science, Babette told Trish Matthews and Carly Poptart that she liked them but would not give up her other friends to be their friend. Then she tucked her assignment lists in her science folder.

By the end of the day, Babette had broken the hearts of four boys, ignored the attention of several popular girls, and filed away assignments for English, math, science, social studies, and band. She ran home as fast as she could, went to her room, closed her door, and got out all of her folders. She lined them up on her bed and started to cry. Beauregard came out from under her bed, where he'd been sleeping.

Arts and Crafts Tip:
For Each Class, Have a Notebook and Folder in the Same Color

The next important step to getting organized for school is to have one folder and one notebook for each class. Try to make the folder and notebook the same color. For example, for English, have a green notebook and a green folder. For math, a blue notebook and a blue folder. This way, when you are in a hurry and you're getting your notebook and folder out of your locker, you won't get the wrong notebook or folder. Also, write the subject in BIG BLOCK LETTERS on the front of each, like so:

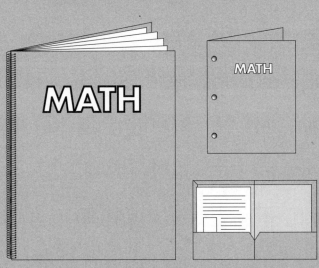

You also want to make sure you have one three-ring binder to hold your personal schedule (which we'll discuss later in the chapter), blank notebook paper, and other miscellaneous documents that may apply to more than one class. Keep this binder with you at all times.

Now—and this is important—write your name, your locker number, and your home phone number on the inside of the front cover of each of your notebooks and folders. This way, if you leave a notebook or folder on the bus or in study hall, whoever finds it can get it back to you pronto.

"And what is the matter?" he asked her.

"Oh, Beauregard. I did just like I had to. I really started off the year well. I got all my assignments, I put them all in separate folders, I turned down the attentions of many, many people so I'd have enough time for my schoolwork, and what do I have now? A big pile of papers I don't know what to do with . . . that's what! There is so much to do and so little time. I do not know where to start. I am doomed! I will never, ever be Felton Jack's fashion designer!"

"I am a cat," said Beauregard, licking his tail. "I have nothing to do all day except sleep and eat and clean myself, so I really don't know anything about organizing time. But, I do not think you are doomed. I think there is someone you know who can help you."

"Who?"

"Barnaby."

"You are right!" screamed Babette. "He is the smartest person I know! He must be organized!"

Babette and Beauregard rushed back to Mellman Middle School. They found Barnaby outside the building typing on his laptop computer.

"I think I've got it!" he exclaimed at the top of his squeaky voice.

"What do you have?" asked Babette.

"Only a magic potion that will allow people to travel great distances in seconds, that's all," said Barnaby.

"Magic potion? That sounds like trouble," warned Beauregard, who had been dragged along on enough of Barnaby's wacky adventures already. He scatted off down the sidewalk as fast as his paws could take him.

"Barnaby, a magic potion, that is wonderful. Do not listen to that ornery cat," said Babette. "But listen to me, I need your help." So Babette told Barnaby about her dream to design clothes for Felton Jack. She then explained her realization that she needed to do well in school and told him how she bought separate folders for each class and how her teachers gave her all these different schedules and assignments that she didn't know what to do with now that she had them.

"I can't help you, Babette," snapped Barnaby, closing his laptop computer and storing it in his hair. "I'm sorry. I have to prepare for class tomorrow, and I have to get my hair cut." Babette, more frustrated than ever, ran off, sobbing. Beauregard, who had witnessed this exchange from his perch in a tree, jumped down and whipped Barnaby with his tail.

"She really needs your help. You're being selfish," said Beauregard. "Can't you take your nose out of your laptop long enough to help a friend in need?"

"None of your beeswax, cat," Barnaby retorted, feeling bad because he realized he had been behaving selfishly. With that he started running—an activity he usually chose to avoid—after Babette screaming, "Please, wait up!"

Barnaby finally caught up to Babette.

"Don't cry," said Barnaby.

"Why not?" she sobbed. "I give up. I am through. Finished. Stick a fork in me. I am done."

Barnaby held Babette's head to his lab coat. His collection of ball-point pens pressed into her cheek. His heart swelled.

"Please don't cry. You're scaring me."

"You're scared?" she said, looking into his deep, green eyes, protected by thick lenses. "How do you think I feel? I will never get into Fashion High if you do not help me get organized.

Felton Jack needs a talented, compassionate French designer now that Kiki Krayola has passed on to the great runway in the sky!"

"Babette, listen to me," pleaded Barnaby. "Studying has never been a problem for me because I've never studied a single minute. I'm a supergenius, remember? That's why I'm already a teacher in your school, even though we're the same age."

Babette cried some more.

"So I wouldn't be much help giving advice on how to get organized," he continued.

"But I need help now," said Babette. "I've got soccer practice starting next Tuesday, trumpet lessons every Thursday, the big shoe sale on Eighth Street is next Thursday, and the VH-1 Fashion Awards are rerun on television every other night. And now all this homework!"

"Sounds like you've got a lot going on," said Barnaby, pondering the situation. Being a supergenius, Barnaby came up with an excellent idea, "I know! How about we go see Bridget? She's great at organizing stuff."

Babette looked up, brow scrunched. "But she's still in London working at her summer job, managing Grandson's 'Young As I Wanna Be' European tour. She won't be back until the third week of class."

"No problem," said Barnaby, and from his glorious, disheveled mass of hair pulled his laptop on which he had written the formula for his potion. "I've been working on a potion that dissolves people and animals into fine particles that are then carried by the wind to any location on the planet in a matter of seconds," he explained. "Let's go to my house and mix up a batch. We need to mix three vials of toothpaste with fluoride with equal parts of Oil of Olay and cat hair to land in London, England."

"Oh, Barnaby, thank you," said Babette, grabbing his skinny hand. "If I don't have the grades to get into Fashion High,

Tip about Annoying Geniuses:
Some People Don't Need to Study Too Much

There are probably people in your class who seem to do really well in school without lifting a pencil or paying attention to *anything* the teacher says. If you aren't one of those people, don't worry about it. There will always be Barnaby-like supergeniuses around, but most of us have to study to do well. If you try to act like the Barnabys of the world and don't study, you've found a great way to end up with very, very bad grades. If a friend of yours gets good grades, but never seems to try very hard, he might be working harder than he lets on, but even if he isn't, you'll only hurt yourself if you try to copy his bad study habits.

Felton Jack is doomed. You know he's been knighted. Just like Sir Lancelot and Sir Paul McCartney."

"Yes, I know that," said Barnaby. "I am a supergenius."

"Beauregard!" called Babette, looking around for him. She spotted that charmer on the corner, flirting with a cute little calico cat. "We have to get to Barnaby's house, *tout suite*. Bring your new friend."

"Yes, *tout suite*," declared Beauregard. Turning to his friend, he said, "That's French for 'very fast.'"

"Meow," purred the calico cat.

"Indeed," said Beauregard. "Let's join them. May I call you 'Brenda'?"

"Meow," agreed the calico cat.

So Babette and Barnaby and Beauregard and Brenda trotted off to Barnaby's apartment on the nineteenth floor of a seventy-two-story building. Barnaby's mother and father were at work, she developing a higher fructose corn syrup, he painting billboards, so the kids and the cats had the place to themselves.

"Nice place," said Babette. "Why have you never invited me here before?"

"Because I'm shy and afraid of girls," said Barnaby.

"That is sweet, dear Barnaby," said Babette. "Can I have something to drink?"

"Sure, go into the fridge. Look on my mom's vanity for her bottle of Oil of Olay and bring it to me. I'll get the toothpaste. Now we just need some cat hair."

"Don't look at me!" hissed Beauregard. "And don't you dare look at fair Brenda, you vile hair harvester!"

"Come on Beauregard," begged Barnaby. "I need cat hair for this to work."

"Ours is currently in use, if you haven't noticed."

Babette returned from the kitchen.

"Can you convince Beauregard to give up some of his oh-so-valuable cat hair, Babette?" asked Barnaby.

"There is no need for me to convince him. Beauregard let me in on a little secret earlier today. When people use slang words, he has an involuntary reaction of coughing up hairballs."

"Noooooooooo!" screamed Beauregard, but it was too late. Babette was on a slang roll, spouting off phrases that made Beauregard nauseated.

Beauregard coughed up great gobs of hair.

"That was the worst slang I ever heard," said Barnaby.

"I am French," said Babette. "It is the best I could do from watching your American television."

With the key ingredients together, Barnaby mixed his potion and poured a quarter-size puddle of it into everyone's hand.

"Now everyone, rub the potion on your nose," said Barnaby. They all did, and they dissolved into fine particles. Then a wind took them from Barnaby's apartment in New York City to London, England.

Just as they landed in front of Big Ben, the famous British clock, each of them miraculously turned from particles back into their natural figures.

"That was really, really cool!" exclaimed Beauregard.

"Yeah," said Babette.

"Meow," said the calico cat.

"Now we have to find Bridget," said Babette. "Barnaby, call Ticketmaster, see where Grandson is playing tonight."

"I'm on it," said Barnaby, as he pulled a cellular phone from his hair. "Hello, Ticketmaster? Yes, I want to know where The Grandsons are playing tonight. What? The Grandsons. What? Oh, *Grandson*, I see. They are called *Grandson*. Thank you."

"They're at the Royal Albert Hall!" said Barnaby, and they all rubbed more potion on their noses and were transported on English winds to the famous concert hall.

Bridget was in the hospitality room, talking on *her* cellular phone.

"Oh Ihop, you are *so* funny. You've got to tell me more of your funny, funny jokes later tonight! You should be a comedian! Bye-bye." She closed her phone and sighed.

"Hey, Bridget," said Barnaby.

"Barnaby! Babette! Beauregard!" exclaimed Bridget. "What are you doing here?"

"And Brenda," corrected Beauregard, introducing his Calico friend.

"And Brenda!" said Bridget. "So nice to meet you. And so nice of you guys to pop in! How did you find me?"

Babette explained, "We all used this potion Barnaby invented that made us dissolve into tiny particles and float on the wind to, *voila*, arrive here—in London. Then I called Ticketmaster to find out where Grandson was playing."

"*Voila* means 'There it is' in French," said Beauregard to Brenda.

"Meow," said the calico cat.

"And who exactly is this 'The Grandsons' band?" asked Beauregard.

"*Grandson* is only the biggest selling pop group *ever*," said Bridget. "Three teenage brothers? All have blond hair? Really cute? They sing the song 'Good Guy Groove.' Ring a bell?"

"No," said Beauregard. "I'm more into hip hop myself. Puff Daddy. Coolio. Mariah Carey on her *Butterfly* album."

"And you don't like slang?" asked Babette.

"I am a mass of contradictions," replied Beauregard.

"Meow," said the calico cat.

"So how is the tour going?" asked Barnaby.

"Like clockwork," said Bridget.

"How do you keep it all together?" asked Babette.

"One word," said Bridget. "Schedules."

"Yes!" screamed Babette, startling Bridget. "Barnaby was right! See Bridget, the reason we came to see you is that I need to do really well in school this year so I can become Felton Jack's fashion designer."

"Of course," said Bridget.

"Yes," said Barnaby, "and since you are so organized, we thought you'd be great at showing Babette how to get organized, so she can study and do well in school."

"No problem. See, Babette, I use a schedule to keep Grandson's 'Young As I Wanna Be' European tour on track just like I use schedules to keep myself on track at school. Here, let me show you today's Grandson schedule."

Time of Day	
Name: Bridget	**Date:** Tuesday

Time of Day	
6 a.m.	
7 a.m.	Wake Ihop for his yoga class
8 a.m.	Wake Thack and Sailor
9 a.m.	Boys have breakfast with parents
10 a.m.	BBC Channel 3 interview (Ihop only)
11 a.m.	Teen Beat photo shoot (Thack and Sailor)
noon	Home schooling (all 3) Buy bologna and cheese for pre-concert meet and greet
1 p.m.	Lunch (all 3)
2 p.m.	Hair appointment (all 3)
3 p.m.	Sailor's tambourine lesson, Thack's drum lesson Make goo-goo eyes at Ihop so he knows I like him
4 p.m.	Naptime (Thack and Sailor)
5 p.m.	Late tea with Queen Elizabeth (all 3) Make goo-goo eyes at Ihop so he knows I like him
6 p.m.	Soundcheck at Royal Albert Hall (all 3)
7 p.m.	Pre-concert meet and greet (all 3)
8 p.m.	RAH concert
9 p.m.	
10 p.m.	Speed away from concert in limousine (all 3)
11 p.m.	Thack and Sailor bedtime
midnight	Ihop bedtime

"Wow, how do you do all this, Bridget?" asked Barbaby. "Even I, a supergenius with weird hair that I can store things in, would have a hard time keeping all this straight."

"You definitely need a schedule," replied Bridget. "The problem is, as you can see, I'm really busy on Tuesday, so I won't have time to make my schedule for Wednesday."

"I will do it!" exclaimed Babette. "Can I? Can I? I need the practice."

"No problem, Babs!" said Bridget, and pulled out of her pocket a huge handful of wadded up paper. "Here are all the things I have to get organized for Wednesday. If you could just write them in my daily planner, I'd really appreciate it. Look back at Tuesday's entries when you're doing it. It might make these scribblings more clear."

"Thanks!" said Babette, taking Bridget's pile of notes. "And never, ever call me Babs." Then she got to work.

Bedtime (all 3)
10 pm

Regis and Kathie Lee,
Live in LONDON – 10 am
(just Thack)

Noon – private tutoring
(Thop & Sailor)

3 pm – School (Thop)

Wake Thop for yoga class – 7am

Sailor eye exam – 3 pm

Thack drums – 3 pm

Appointment with chiropractor
(me and Thop) 5 pm

Naptime – 4 pm all 3

Yoga class (me) 4 pm

Sailor tambourine 11 am

2:00 pm –
pick up matching
costumes for the
band at dry cleaners

7 pm –
soundcheck
at London
Children's Hospital

8 pm – Surprise gig
at London
Children's Hospital

Wake Thack and Sailor – 8 am

9 pm –
speed away
IN limousine

1 pm –
serve protein – enriched
health shakes

MTV style Interview
Thack and Sailor – 6 pm

QUICK QUIZ 1

Arrange Bridget's Appointments on This Daily Planner Page

Name:	Date:
Time of Day	
6 a.m.	
7 a.m.	
8 a.m.	
9 a.m.	
10 a.m.	
11 a.m.	
noon	
1 p.m.	
2 p.m.	
3 p.m.	
4 p.m.	
5 p.m.	
6 p.m.	
7 p.m.	
8 p.m.	
9 p.m.	
10 p.m.	
11 p.m.	
midnight	

See page 146 for Quick Quiz 1 answers.

When Babette finished, she gave the schedule back to Bridget.

"Thanks, Babette. This looks great. Now, will you fill out my personal schedule for the rest of the tour?"

"What?" exclaimed Babette. "That daily planner took me long enough."

"I know, but this won't take much longer. All you need to do is fill in my routine for next week—the things I have to do every day at the same time for the rest of the tour. It's what I call my 'Personal Schedule'—the things I do every day."

"I don't get it," said Babette, miffed.

"Okay. Let's see if I can explain. Is there a group of things you have to do every week?"

"Yes," said Babette, hesitantly.

"Like what?"

"Well, I go to school every day at the same time and leave at the same time."

"Good."

"I have trumpet lessons every Thursday," Babette continued, "and soccer practice on Tuesday."

"Right. These are the things you do every week at the same time. I have things I have to do every week, too, like wake up the boys, get them to music lessons, make sure they show up for home schooling. That's *my* personal schedule."

"Okay. I see. I think". said Babette.

"I tell you what. Take a look at my personal schedule from the last tour I managed for The Space Grrrls. These are the things I did every week at the exact same time on The Space Grrrls' tour of Japan."

Time of Day	Monday	Tuesday	Wednesday	Thursday	Friday
6 a.m.					
7 a.m.					
8 a.m.					
9 a.m.	wake up the SGs	wake up the SGs	wake up the SGs	wake up the SGs	wake up the SGs
10 a.m.					
11 a.m.	get the SGs to aerobics class	get the SGs to aerobics class	get the SGs to aerobics class	get the SGs to aerobics class	get the SGs to aerobics class
12 p.m.					
1 p.m.	Outer Space voice lesson		Outer Space voice lesson		Outer Space voice lesson
2 p.m.	SGs eat lunch at Arby's	SGs eat lunch at Burger King	SGs eat lunch at McDonalds	SGs eat lunch at Hardees	SGs eat lunch at Wendy's
3 p.m.					
4 p.m.	SGs have hair and makeup done	SGs have hair and makeup done	SGs have hair and makeup done	SGs have hair and makeup done	SGs have hair and makeup done
5 p.m.					
6 p.m.					
7 p.m.					
8 p.m.					

Dates: Jan. 2 – Jan. 6

Personal Schedule of Bridget

"I think I understand," said Babette. "These are the things you do at the same time every week. Then, once you have your personal schedule written down, you can just add to it as things come up.

"Exactly," replied Bridget. "You are really getting the hang of things now."

"Thank you," said Babette.

"So here are my daily tasks now—the stuff I do the at the same time every day of the week on Grandson's European tour. If you write them down on this weekly schedule, I can photocopy it and use it for the rest of the tour."

QUICK QUIZ 2

Fill Out Bridget's Personal Schedule

Arrange Bridget's daily tasks on this weekly schedule.

Bridget's Daily Tasks

5 p.m.	make goo-goo eyes at Ihop
7 a.m.	wake Ihop for yoga class
8 a.m.	wake Thack and Sailor
3 p.m.	Thack drum lesson, Sailor tambourine lesson
9 a.m.	breakfast with parents
12 to 1 p.m.	home schooling for the band

Serve protein-enriched health shakes 9 a.m., 1 p.m., 8 p.m.

Naptime for Thack and Sailor—4 p.m.

Dates:			Personal Schedule of _____		
Time of Day	**Monday**	**Tuesday**	**Wednesday**	**Thursday**	**Friday**
6 a.m.					
7 a.m.					
8 a.m.					
9 a.m.					
10 a.m.					
11 a.m.					
12 p.m.					
1 p.m.					
2 p.m.					
3 p.m.					
4 p.m.					
5 p.m.					
6 p.m.					
7 p.m.					
8 p.m.					

See page 147 for Quick Quiz 2 answers.

"Bridget?" asked Babette.

"Yes?" replied Bridget.

"Where are Barnaby, Beauregard, and Brenda?"

The three had slipped out unnoticed from Bridget's office.

"Oh jeez, I hope they aren't getting into any trouble," said Bridget. "That's the last thing I need."

"Hey, Bridget," said Babette. "Forget about them. Are you done making me do all your work yet? I have written down your daily schedule for Tuesday and your personal schedule—the stuff you do at the same time every week—for the rest of the tour."

"Babette, this is all good training."

"For what?"

"For school, silly girl."

"Don't ever call me silly girl."

"Sorry," Bridget apologized. "Jeez, you are touchy. I'm having you help me with my tour schedules so you can start making your own schedules for school."

"I see," said Babette. "So my school schedule will be a lot like your tour schedule?"

"Yes. Now, let's start with your class schedule."

"I already have a class schedule. It's a computer printout I got the first day of school."

"I know," said Bridget. "Let me see it."

"Great," said Bridget, taking the schedule. "This is just like the personal schedule you did for me."

"No, it's not," Babette disagreed. "This one's all jumbled up."

```
Babette's Class Schedule

Band               9:00        TTh
English            9:00        MWF
Gym               11:00        MWF
Homeroom           8:00        MTWThF
Lunch             11:00        TTh
                  12:00        MWF
Math              10:00        MTWThF
Science            1:00        MTWThF
Social Studies    12:00        TTh
                   2:00        MWF
Study Hall         2:00        TTh
```

"Well, it's kind of jumbled up, I guess. It's in alphabetical order. What you need to do is copy these down onto a chronological schedule, and you'll be set. Here, take this blank chronological schedule and copy down your classes."

"Wait," said Babette. "What does 'chronological' mean?"

"It means 'in the order of the time when events occur.' You know, putting things in the order that they happen, like English first at 9 a.m., math second at 10 a.m., science third at 11 a.m."

"Got it," said Babette.

From ABCs to 123s Tip:
Turn Alphabetical Schedules into Chronological Schedules

Schedules are easier to read if they are ordered chronologically instead of alphabetically. If your schedule is listed alphabetically, turn it into a chronological schedule as soon as possible. Although your classes may not be the same as Babette's, you can still organize your personal schedule in the same way she did. Just fill in your own classes and activities in the appropriate times and dates.

QUICK QUIZ 3

Create a Class Schedule

Use the computer printout of Babette's Class Schedule to fill in the blank school schedule below.

Dates:			Personal Schedule of _____		
Time of Day	**Monday**	**Tuesday**	**Wednesday**	**Thursday**	**Friday**
6 a.m.					
7 a.m.					
8 a.m.					
9 a.m.					
10 a.m.					
11 a.m.					
12 p.m.					
1 p.m.					
2 p.m.					
3 p.m.					
4 p.m.					
5 p.m.					
6 p.m.					
7 p.m.					
8 p.m.					

See page 148 for Quick Quiz 3 answers.

"Now, with this chronological class schedule, you'll be able to make it to class on time."

"Promptness has always has been a problem for me, I'll admit," Babette revealed.

"And now this is the base for your personal schedule," explained Bridget.

"It is?"

"Yes. All you need to do is add to this schedule activities you'll be doing at the same time every week, like trumpet lessons.

"Thursdays at 3:30," said Babette, and added it to her personal schedule.

"Anything else?"

"I've got soccer practice Tuesdays and Thursdays at 5 p.m.," said Babette, adding it to her personal schedule, "and that's about it. Oh, and 'VH1 Fashion TV,' every Wednesday, 7 to 9 p.m. Very important if I am to become Felton Jack's personal fashion designer."

				3:30–4:00 trumpet lesson	
3 p.m.					
After School					
4 p.m.					
5 p.m.	Soccer practice			Soccer practice	
6 p.m.					
7 p.m.		7:00–9:00 VH1 Fashion TV			
8 p.m.		↓			

"Great. Now give me your personal schedule so we can have copies of it made," said Bridget, calling "Barnaby? Barnaby!"

"Yes?" he said, running in with a guitar in one hand and a tambourine in the other.

"Be a dear. Put down Grandson's instruments, run to the copier, and make twenty copies of this."

"Okay," he said. "But first, I'm thinking of combining the tambourine and the guitar to make a whole new instrument. I'll remove the tambourine's castanets, place strings over across the drum so the tambourine drum is like the body of the guitar, with a neck stuck on it."

"You mean a banjo?" said Babette.

"Oh yeah," said Barnaby. "That's a banjo, isn't it?"

"Okay, people, let's focus here!" said Bridget. "Barnaby is now going to make twenty photocopies of Babette's personal schedule. Go! Shoo! Twenty copies will last you twenty weeks—*much* longer than one semester of school, just in case you need extras."

"Thanks, Bridget, this is great!" exclaimed Babette.

Arts and Crafts:
Make Your Own Personal Schedule

You can make a personal schedule to keep your life—and your schoolwork—organized.

Step 1: Make a couple photocopies of the blank weekly schedule in the back of this book (page162).

Step 2: Fill one in with your weekly personal schedule including:

★ Your class schedule

★ Other things you do the same time every week, like music lessons and team practices

(Tip: Fill it in with a pencil. You will probably make a few mistakes or have to change a few things.)

Step 3: Take this personal schedule page and photo-copy it twenty times.

Step 4: Get a full-year calendar. Write the dates in your personal schedule for each week.

Step 5: Put your personal schedule in your three-ring binder that you keep with you all the time, which we discussed earlier in the chapter.

"No problem," said Bridget. "But we're not done yet."

"Oh no," said Babette. "Do you need me to do more of your work for you?"

"Very funny," said Bridget. "This is what I get for trying to help? Abuse from you?"

"No. I am sorry. Go ahead."

"I will. Now, we are going to add your assignments and tests to your handy-dandy personal schedule. Do you have the folders for all of your classes with you?"

"Yes. Here in my backpack."

"Good. What do you have first period?"

"English, with Mr. Blister."

"Ugh. You got Blister? He's tough, but don't worry, get your English folder and get out Blister's handouts."

English   Mr. Blister

Week 1 Assignments

Wednesday: One-page report on what I
     did over my summer vacation.
Friday: Test on first twenty pages of
     Of Mice and Men.

"Now, what you're going to do is add these English assignments to your personal schedule."

"But I don't have to do these every week," Babette reminded Bridget.

"I know, you just add these to week one of your personal schedule on the one day they are due."

Barnaby returned with twenty photocopies of Babette's personal schedule.

"Here you go," he said. "Those British copy machines are weird. You put the paper on the right side instead of the left side, and . . ."

"Whatever." said Bridget, dismissing Barnaby. "Okay, Babette. Write 'Week 1' and the dates on the first page of your personal schedule, and add your English assignments to it."

"Cool. Now I won't forget!"

"You may forget," said Bridget. "But if you look at your schedule every day, it will remind you. That's what it's there for."

"This sure seems like a lot of work, Bridget. Plus I still have all my schoolwork to do!"

"It does take a while to get your personal schedule together," agreed Bridget, "but once that's done, all you are doing is writing in your daily assignments and your test dates. *That* takes only a few minutes."

"So, now I just write down my assignments for all my other classes?"

"Yes."

Babette got out her math assignments for that week, and her science assignments, and her personal schedule.

Quick Quiz 4

Babette's Personal Schedule

Enter the following tests and assignments to Babette's Week 2 personal schedule.

Science:	Thursday—hand in lab report on fruit fly experiment
Math:	Wednesday—hand in exercises 1.1 and 1.2
	Friday—read through p. 25
Gym:	Friday—ten pull-ups
English:	Monday—read through chapter 2 of *Of Mice and Men*
	Friday—quiz on *Of Mice and Men*, through chapter 3
Social Studies:	Tuesday—read section 1.3
	Friday—read section 1.4

Dates: Week One			Personal Schedule of _Babette_		
Time of Day	**Monday**	**Tuesday**	**Wednesday**	**Thursday**	**Friday**
6 a.m.					
7 a.m.					
8 a.m.	Homeroom	Homeroom	Homeroom	Homeroom	Homeroom
9 a.m.	English	Band	English	Band	English
10 a.m.	Math	Math	Math	Math	Math
11 a.m.	Gym	Lunch	Gym	Lunch	Gym
12 p.m.	Lunch	Social Studies	Lunch	Social Studies	Lunch
1 p.m.	Science	Science	Science	Science	Science
2 p.m.	Social Studies	Study Hall	Social Studies	Study Hall	Social Studies
3 p.m.					
4 p.m.					
5 p.m.					
6 p.m.					
7 p.m.					
8 p.m.					

See page 149 for Quick Quiz 4 answers.

More Work Now, Less Work Later Tip: Make Making Your Personal Schedule Part of Your Week 1 Homework

If you include creating your personal schedule as part of your homework for the first week of the school year, you'll be ahead of the game for the rest of the semester. If your school year is already underway, don't wait until next semester or next year to start your schedule. Just start it from wherever you are in the school year and go from there.

"What about these year-long and first-semester schedules that some teachers hand out? Should I just file those away and not worry about them?"

"Look at your year-long and one-semester schedules. Do they have any important dates on them, like when a big test is, or when a big paper is due?"

"Some of them do. There's a big exam in social studies on October twelfth on the sixties. I don't even know what the sixties *is.*"

"I don't either, but you will by October twelfth, so go ahead and turn to your personal schedule for October twelfth and write down 'exam on the sixties.' Now, do the same with the rest of your classes in which the teacher gave you schedules for later assignments."

As Babette filled in her personal schedule, a strange presence filled the room.

"Hey Bridget!" said a blond youngster.

"Ihop!" said Bridget, checking her schedule. "It's 5:30! Why aren't you at late tea with the Queen?

"Just was," said Ihop. "Thack and Sailor are still there. She's telling them a story about getting a pony when she was our age. Booooring. I excused myself. Had to practice a new solo I'm working on for the show tonight."

"Oh, okay," said Bridget. "Ihop Grandson, I want you to meet my French friend, Babette."

"Nice to meet you, Babs!" said Ihop.

"And you," said Babette. "But my name is not . . ."

"France, eh?" interrupted Ihop "We just got back from there. Played six sold-out shows at the Louvre Museum gift shop. You like mayonnaise on your french fries, Babs, like the rest of France does?"

"My name is Babette," she corrected, "and yes, I love mayonnaise on my french fries."

"Cool! Well, you guys invented french fries and all, so I guess you're the experts, right?" said Ihop, a little nervous because

Babette is so pretty. "Um, Bridget. I came over here because, see, when I was practicing my new solo, I broke all the strings on my guitar. I was really rocking out. Can you find me a new set of strings?"

"I'm on it," said Bridget, assuming her tour-manager tone of voice. "Ihop, you go round up Sailor and Thack, and Babette and I will meet you in your dressing room in fifteen minutes with six shiny new strings."

"Cool!" said Ihop. "Thanks! I'll go get my brothers. Maybe the Queen is done talking about horses by now. Nice to meet you, Babette."

"And you," said Babette.

"Okay Babette," said Bridget, "Do you think you're ready for school now?"

"Definitely."

"Good. Here are free passes to tonight's show for you and Barnaby and Beauregard and Brenda. Have a great time, and I'll see you when I get back from the tour."

"Will do," replied Babette. "Barnaby! Beauregard! Brenda!"

Babette wandered around the backstage of the Royal Albert Hall, looking for her friends. She found them in the hospitality room, stuffing themselves with free bologna sandwiches. With them was none other than Felton Jack, dressed in a tight-fitting, shiny gold jogging suit.

"Mr. Jack!" exclaimed Babette. "What on earth are you wearing?"

"Mmmpph?" he said, chewing away. "Mmmpph mmmpph mmmpph."

"You're in worse fashion shape than I thought," said Babette, taking the sandwich tray away from the ravenous pop star. "But don't worry. Now that I know how to make schedules and plan my school days, I am that much closer to being your personal fashion designer!"

Felton Jack smiled and hugged her. Crumbs from his mouth fell down the back of her shirt. They all left together to watch Grandson rock out at Royal Albert Hall.

Grandson played four songs.

"Thank you, England!" yelled Sailor. "It's past our bedtime, so we must go!"

The fans went bananas, screaming for more. But Grandson had already performed three encores, so they scattered.

"Quick!" yelled Barnaby, scared of the enormous screaming crowd. "Rub the last of the potion on your nose and think of my apartment!"

Babette, Beauregard, and Brenda obeyed and before they knew it, they were back in New York City in Barnaby's parents' apartment . . . with Barnaby's parents.

"What in *Sam Hill*?" yelled Barnaby's dad, Fred.

"Holy heck!" yelled Barnaby's mom, Frieda.

"Hi Mom, hi Dad," said Barnaby sheepishly. "These are my friends."

"*Never mind* who these people and *cats* are son," said Fred. "What are you all doing appearing *out of thin air* in the middle of the *living room*?"

"New potion," explained Barnaby. "Basically, it makes you disappear, then reappear elsewhere. Nothing special."

"Well, where did you just reappear from, son?" asked Frieda.

"London!" said Babette.

"England?" asked Fred.

"No, *France*," said Beauregard, sarcastically.

"Meow," said the calico cat.

Fred was not amused.

"Just you *wait* a minute. First you come *reappearing* in our living room from London," said Fred, "and *then* I have to get *guff* from a talking cat with an *attitude*? Is *that* how it is these days? *Barnaby*? Are these the *kind of mammals* you *hang out* with? Answer me!"

"Yes, sir," said Barnaby.

"Barnaby," said Frieda. "Please ask your friends to leave. We have a lot of talking to do young man, a lot of talking."

"But Ma!" pleaded Barnaby.

"Don't 'but Ma' me!" cautioned Frieda. "The last thing I want to see after a long day of inventing a higher fructose corn syrup is my only son appearing out of thin air in the middle of my living room! From London, England, no less!"

"And *the last thing* I want to see after painting billboards all day is *my son* appearing out of *thin air* in the middle *of my living room* with a cat with a *bad attitude*," added Fred.

"Sorry guys," said Barnaby. "I guess you have to go. I'll see you tomorrow in school Babette."

"Thanks for your help," said Babette. "And I'm sorry. Please don't be mad at Barnaby. He was only trying to help me become Felton Jack's fashion designer."

"What in *Sam Hill* is she *talking about*, Barnaby?" asked Fred.

"Nothing, Dad."

"Barnaby?" asked Frieda.

"Yes, Mom?'

"Have you seen my Oil of Olay?"

Babette, Beauregard, and Brenda walked back to Babette's house. It was early evening. Men and women were leaving work; children were in their sports uniforms on their way to soccer and baseball games; and cats were in doorways of restaurants, dry cleaners, and grocery stores, meowing and cleaning themselves.

"With this new schedule, I really think I'm going to keep my life organized," said Babette.

"I hope so," said Beauregard, winking at a cute tabby, to Brenda's dismay. "That gold jumpsuit that Felton Jack was wearing was the worst outfit I've seen since Sylvester the Cat dressed up like a Grandma to get Tweety Bird."

"Meow," meowed the cute tabby to Beauregard. Brenda waddled over and gave the unsuspecting tabby a terrifying hiss.

"HHHHHsssssssssKKKKsssssshhhhhssssiiissss!" hissed Brenda.

The tabby ran away.

"You said it," said Babette. "So, after all that traveling, what day is it?"

"It's still Monday," said Beauregard. "First day of school."

"Great!" exclaimed Babette. "'Melrose Place' is on tonight!"

"In five minutes!" yelled Beauregard, and they all ran as fast as they could to Babette's apartment to watch their favorite TV show.

Quick Summary of Chapter 3

★ Make doing well in school your first priority.

★ Keep materials from each class in separate folders.

★ Transform the computerized class schedule you get into your own chronological schedule.

★ Make a weekly personal schedule using the weekly schedule in the back of this book (page 162). Put on it the things you do at the same time every week, like going to school, music lessons, etc. Make copies of your personal schedule and put it in your three-ring binder, which you should keep with you at all times.

★ Add assignments and test dates to the personal schedule when your teachers tell you about them.

★ Also add to your personal schedule big tests and papers that your teachers tell you about far in advance, and add any dates that are on a semester- or year-long schedule that they have passed out to the class.

Chapter 4
Taking Notes in Class

TUESDAY

Babette woke up, showered, dressed, ate a breakfast of French toast and grapefruit, and went to school.

"Hey, Babette," said Shane Fusselman. "Did you get started on *Of Mice and Men*?"

"Yeah," she said. "I read the first ten pages after 'Melrose Place' last night."

"Pretty good, wasn't it?"

"Yeah. When Michael Mancini socked Dr. Peter Burns because Peter stole his gal, that was really cool."

"I meant the book," explained Shane. "The book is really good."

"Oh yeah right, the book, it's fine."

"You know we have that test on it Friday."

"I do know that. I wrote it down in my personal schedule when I was in London, before I went to see Grandson play."

"Huh?"

"Long story."

"So, you're ready for the test?"

"Well, I will be," said Babette.

"Shane! Babette!" said Mr. Blister. "Please, stop gossiping and be quiet. Now, class, let's discuss *Of Mice and Men*."

Mr. Blister started talking and Shane started scribbling.

"Psst," whispered Babette. "Shane. What are you doing?"

"Taking notes," Shane whispered back.

"Oh."

Notes. Something Babette had heard of and even tried to take but had never quite mastered. In the rest of her classes, she saw others taking notes: Bobby in math, Carly and Trish in history. But no one ever really explained to Babette how to take notes.

Huge Mega-Important Note-Taking Tip: The Secrets to Taking Good Notes

Anyone can scribble away while the teacher is talking. Taking good notes, on the other hand, relies on the following three mega-important things.

1. Be Neat.

Notes are reminders to you of what the teacher said in class, so for them to work, you need to be neat. Even if you think the teacher is going too fast, and it's hard to get everything down, try to write neatly because you won't be able to remember *anything* your teacher said if you can't read what you wrote.

2. Listen Carefully.

To avoid frantically scribbling everything the teacher says is to listen carefully for the important stuff. The teacher often tips you off on important stuff by saying things like:

"The three reasons for that are . . ."

"The main point is . . ."

"You should remember that . . ."

and

"This will be on the test."

Another way to figure out the important stuff to write down is to ask yourself questions about the material being covered in class. (Note: It is best to ask these questions to yourself. If you ask them out loud, your classmates may look at you funny.)

For example, if your social studies class is studying Abraham Lincoln and the teacher is talking about her trip to Bermuda, you probably don't need to be taking notes on Bermuda. Keep asking yourself:

"Why is this important?"

"Who or what are we talking about?"

"Where and when did this or will this take place?"

"What is the teacher's main point?"

"How is this related to the course topic?"

"What are the relevant dates, sources, or equations I need to remember?"

If you can answer any of these kinds of questions, it's probably important enough to write in your notes.

3. When the Teacher Changes the Subject, You Change the Subject.

When something new is being discussed, draw a line across the page to show in your notes that the teacher changed the subject in class. Leave a few spaces above the line in case the teacher backtracks. That way you can write more notes above the line about the previous topic. Like this:

Abraham Lincoln lived in Illinois, Indiana, and Kentucky as a boy.
Abe was a lawyer.

_____

John Wilkes Booth
He shot Lincoln in the Ford Theater.
He was an actor.

If possible, write a new heading for the new stuff the teacher is talking about. When you go back to revise your notes, it will make it that much easier to see where one topic leaves off and another begins.

What does "revise your notes" mean, you ask? Read on.

topic (*n.*) a subject of discussion or conversation.

At the end of the day, Babette had taken notes in all her classes. She went home. She opened her English notebook. It was a mess.

"*Sacre bleu*! What have I done?" she cried. "These notes are so messy. I'm in big trouble. I better call Barnaby again. Looks like we're heading back to Europe."

Chit-Chat Tip:
Make a Few Telebuddies

If Babette knew the phone numbers of a couple people in her class, she wouldn't always have to be calling Barnaby for help. After a few days in school, figure out who you want to be your telebuddies in each class. No, not Teletubbies . . . telebuddies! Exchange phone numbers with your telebuddy so when either of you has a question or forgets something the teacher said, you can call each other.

Barnaby had bad news for his troubled friend.

"Sorry, Babette, I'm out of potion and my mom has hidden her Oil of Olay from me."

"Oh no. Um, any ideas?" she asked.

"Well. Let's see. You need someone to help decipher your notes. Someone who knows *Of Mice and Men* like the back of his hand."

"Or paw," said Babette.

"Huh?"

"Or paw," said Babette. "Beauregard! He's read every book ever written with the word *mice* in it!"

"You know, you're right!" exclaimed Barnaby.

"But he left with Brenda this morning and I have no idea where they went."

"And where does Beauregard go whenever he wants to impress a she-cat?" asked Barnaby.

"Right!" said Babette. "*Cats,* the musical!"

"I'll meet you there," said Barnaby.

They waited outside the Winter Garden Theatre for Beauregard. He came toddling out in his old granny outfit, sobbing, with Brenda, disguised as a distinguished gentleman, beside him. *Cats* did not allow cats, so they had to dress up like people.

"Hi, Beauregard," said Babette. "I had a feeling I'd find you here."

"Yep."

"How was the show?" Barnaby asked.

"Andrew Lloyd Webber has captured the essence of cat," gushed Beauregard. "Our loves, our losses, our natural drowsiness, our need to be clean. Everything!"

"Meow," said Brenda.

"Beauregard, I need your help. Can you skip your usual post-theater prix fixe meal and come home with me? Please? I have ten cans of tuna waiting for you," pleaded Babette.

"Ten cans?" said Beauregard.

"Of your favorite."

"B-B-B-Bumblebee?" asked Beauregard. "Packed in oil?"

"Oui. Bumblebee in oil. Let's go"

"*Oui* means *yes* in French," said Beauregard to Brenda.

"Meow," said Brenda, and they stumbled down Broadway in their costumes.

Beauregard sat down at Babette's to a snack of three cans of tuna fish.

"Now, Beauregard, as you're eating, could you help me decipher my notes on *Of Mice and Men*?"

"A wonderful book, but not really about mice after all," said Beauregard. "I'd rather discuss *Stuart Little*."

Great Book Tip:
Read *Of Mice and Men*

The following exercises and note-taking tips are based on the first chapter of John Steinbeck's great, short book *Of Mice and Men*. The first chapter is about fifteen pages of enthralling, easy reading, so if you want, go to the library or the bookstore, get the book, and read the first chapter. Babette's notes will make more sense.

You don't *have to* read the book—the tips and notes will still make sense—but it's a great book! (For more great books and tips on how to read better, check out another great book published by The Princeton Review, *Reading Smart Junior*.)

"Me, too," agreed Babette. "But we're reading *Of Mice and Men* in English class. I took a bunch of notes, but I need you to help me pick out the important parts."

"Let's have a look."

English

Monday, September 2

John Steinbeck wrote the book Of Mice and Men.

John Steinbeck wrote Of Mice and Men in 1937.

John Steinbeck was born in Salinas, California, in 1902.

John Steinbeck went to Stanford for college
and lived in California for most of his life.

John Steinbeck's first book was Cup of Gold. He wrote it in 1929.

John Steinbeck wrote lots of books. He also wrote The
Grapes of Wrath in 1939 and Travels with Charlie in 1962.

John Steinbeck won the Nobel Prize in 1962. This
was a big year for him.

The Nobel Prize is a big prize they give every year to a
writer. There are also Nobel Prizes for science and peace.

John Steinbeck died in 1968. He lived in New York
when he died.

John Steinbeck is one of America's greatest authors.

John Steinbeck mainly wrote about California's poor people.

He hated how big business and mean rich people made life
hard on poor workers.

Of Mice and Men is about two friends

Grapes of Wrath is about a family in the dustbowl.
It's his most famous book.

Dustbowl — in the 1920s the United States had a drought. It
turned turned the farms in the West into dust. So the
called the West the Dustbowl.

Travels With Charlie — about a man traveling
around the country with his dog.

Write the Date Down Tip:
Always Write the Date Down

The first thing you do when you open your notebook in
class is write down that day's date at the top of the page.
Your notes are much easier to study from this way, and
you can ask your teacher better questions. Your teacher
keeps what she teaches in a dated notebook too.

"These aren't too bad," said Beauregard. "They just need to be *revised* a bit."

"What do you mean 'revised'?" asked Babette.

revise *(v.)* to change and make better.

"You took a ton of notes, and that's good," explained Beauregard. "All you need to do is organize them a little bit. Here, let me show you how I'd do it."

Beauregard sat down with a pencil in his paw.

"What I'm going to do here could change your studying life, so pay attention," advised Beauregard. "See how you took your notes on the left-hand side of your notebook here?"

"Yes."

"Well, from now on, you will *always* take your notes on the left side of your notebook. You will *never* take your notes on the right side of your notebook. You will *always* keep the right-hand page of your notebook blank."

"Why blank?"

Revision Tip #1:
Take Notes on One Side of Your Notebook Only

When you're taking notes, take them on the left side of your notebook. That way, when you go back to revise or study them, you have a blank page right next to your notes to use.

"Because you will be revising your notes on the right-hand side, right across from the notes you took on the left-hand side. Also, if you have a novel or a textbook that you're studying from, you can add stuff from the book to your revised notes on the right side as well."

"Okay, Beauregard."

"The first thing I always do when I revise notes is place some headings," explained Beauregard.

"What are headings?" asked Babette.

"A heading is like a title. Everything that comes under a heading should have something to do with it. For instance, I'll make a heading here called John Steinbeck's Life.

English
   Monday, September 2
      John Steinbeck wrote the book Of Mice and Men.
   John Steinbeck wrote Of Mice and Men in 1937.
✓ John Steinbeck was born in Salinas, California, in 1902.
✓ John Steinbeck went to Stanford for college
      and lived in California for most of his life.
   John Steinbeck's first book was Cup of Gold. He wrote it in 1929.
   John Steinbeck wrote lots of books. He also wrote The
   Grapes of Wrath in 1939 and Travels with Charlie in 1962.
   John Steinbeck won the Nobel Prize in 1962. This
      was a big year for him.
   The Nobel Prize is a big prize they give every year to a
   writer. There are also Nobel Prizes for science and peace.
✓ John Steinbeck died in 1968. He lived in New York
      when he died.
   John Steinbeck is one of America's greatest authors.
   John Steinbeck mainly wrote about California's poor people.
   He hated how big buisness and mean rich people made life
   hard on poor workers.
   Of Mice and Men is about two friends
   Grapes of Wrath is about a family in the dustbowl.
   It's his most famous book.
   Dustbowl — in the 1920s the United States had a drought. It
   turned turned the farms in the West into dust. So the
   called the West the Dustbowl.
      Travels With Charlie — about a man traveling
         around the country with his dog.

John Steinbeck's Life

Born 1902

Born in Salinas, California

Went to college at Stanford in California

Lived in California most of his life

Died 1968

"See, I listed under <u>John Steinbeck's Life</u> all the notes you took that had to do with when he lived and where he lived."

"I see," said Babette.

"Before, these facts were kind of scattered in your notes, probably because the teacher didn't say them all right in a row."

"He didn't. Mr. Blister was all freaked out. He could barely remember his name, much less anything about John Steinbeck. He kept talking about winning the lottery and moving to Bermuda."

"Poor guy. Anyway, as I put some of your notes under <u>John Steinbeck's Life</u>, I checked them off from the left hand side."

> **Revision Tip #2**
>
> Check off your class notes as you revise them. That way you won't put the same thing under two different headings. It also makes you feel good to see things checked off.

"I get it," said Babette. "That way, I won't accidentally write the same notes under different headings. I'll know I already revised the notes that have check marks next to them."

"Exactly."

"So what's next?"

"Next, I make another heading, <u>John Steinbeck's Books</u>."

"Why that heading?"

"If you look at your notes, you can kind of see the different things the teacher talked about. In this class, Mr. Blister talked about John Steinbeck, then he talked about lots of the books he wrote, then he talked about the book you are reading now, *Of Mice and Men*. It looks like most of the notes are about the book *Of Mice and Men* itself, so I want to do that one last." (See Beauregards' notes on page 67)

"Get it?" asked Beauregard.

"I think so. But why did you underline the title of his books?

And why did you circle and star the part about *The Grapes of Wrath*?"

"Good questions, Babette, good questions."

"Do you have answers to my good questions?"

"I do. I underlined the books because that's what the heading is,—John Steinbeck's Books. Most likely, that's what Mr. Blister will cover on a test. I starred and circled *The Grapes of Wrath* because Mr. Blister said that was his best, most important book. He will definitely be asking you about that book someday. Whenever you revise your notes, you want to mark the most important notes with underlines, stars, and circles."

Revision Tip #3

When you revise your notes, underline, circle, and star the most important information. That's the stuff that will be on a test or in your report. If you want to get really scientific about it, you can use different color highlighter markers. You could mark the most important stuff with a green marker, the second most important stuff with pink marker, and the normal important stuff with yellow marker.

"You got it?" asked Beauregard.

"Yes," said Babette.

"Fine. Now, *you* revise your notes from Tuesday's class. Remember, the headings won't be the same for Tuesday, you have to look at the notes and figure out what different topics Mr. Blister discussed in class. I'll be in the kitchen eating tuna. When you're done, give me a yell and I'll have a look-see at your work."

Babette got down to work.

English

Monday, September 2

✓ John Steinbeck wrote the book Of Mice and Men.

✓ John Steinbeck wrote Of Mice and Men in 1937.

✓ John Steinbeck was born in Salinas, California, in 1902.

✓ John Steinbeck went to Stanford for college and lived in California for most of his life.

✓ John Steinbeck's first book was Cup of Gold. He wrote it in 1929.

✓ John Steinbeck wrote lots of books. He also wrote The Grapes of Wrath in 1939 and Travels with Charlie in 1962.

✓ John Steinbeck won the Nobel Prize in 1962. This was a big year for him.

✓ The Nobel Prize is a big prize they give every year to a writer. There are also Nobel Prizes for science and peace.

✓ John Steinbeck died in 1968. He lived in New York when he died. R.I.P.

✓ John Steinbeck is one of America's greatest authors.

✓ John Steinbeck mainly wrote about California's poor people.

✓ He hated how big buisness and mean rich people made life hard on poor workers.

Of Mice and Men is about two friends

✓ Grapes of Wrath is about a family in the dustbowl. It's his most famous book.

✓ Dustbowl — in the 1920s the United States had a drought. It turned turned the farms in the West Into dust. So the called the West the Dustbowl.

✓ Travels With Charlie — about a man traveling around the country with his dog.

John Steinbeck's Life

Born 1902

Born in Salinas, California

Went to college at Stanford in California

Lived in California most of his life

Died 1968

John Steinbeck's Books

JS wrote lots of books.

He is one of America's best writers ever.

His first book was Cup of Gold.

He wrote it in 1929.

He wrote Of Mice and Men in 1937.

It's about 2 brothers.

He wrote The Grapes of Wrath in 1939 (right

after Of Mice and Men), which is about a

family in the Dust Bowl

the West in the 1920s was called the Dust

Bowl because there was a drought.

**The Grapes of Wrath is his most famous

book

He wrote Travels with Charlie in

1962—it's about a man traveling

around the country with his dog.

He wrote mostly about

poor people. He hated how

big business and rich people

treated their poor workers.

He won the Nobel Prize in 1962.

QUICK QUIZ 5

Revise Babette's Notes

Turn to page 70 and revise the notes Babette took in Tuesday's class like Beauregard revised the notes she took in Monday's class. Tuesday's notes are about the book itself, not the author, but the same rules for revising apply. Remember to do the following:

★ List notes under headings.

★ Shorten sentences where you can.

★ Star or underline the really important information.

★ Write everything very neatly.

★ Check off the passages of Babette's notes after you've revised them.

We'll even give you a head start. The headings have already been included on the right side, so all you have to do is figure out where the revised notes should go.

Of Mice and Men was written in 1937 by John Steinbeck
1937 is right before WWII got started.
Mice and Men is about George and Lennie
Are they brothers?
George is the smart one, Lennie is big and dumb.
George is the ~~xxxx~~ leader.
Lennies name is Lennie Small, but he's not small He's huge
Lennie Keeps a mouse in his pocket. George doesn't like the fact that
  Lennie keeps a mouse in his pocket.
Lennie worships George. He does whatever George tells him to do.
There are lots of other TV shows and movies and cartoons based
on Lennie ~~xxx~~ and george.
Lennie and George got run out of Weed (a town). Getting run out means
they were chased out of town by the townsfolk.
Lennie hurt a woman in Weed, but he didn't mean to.
They had to hide in a ditch so they wouldn't get caught by the townspeople.
The took a bus to a new ranch.
Lennie and George are ranch hands.
A ranch hand works on a ranch, he does the hard work on a ranch, like
lifting hay onto a truck and fixing fences and herding cattle.
Lennie and George got off the bus far away from the ranch
they are ~~xxx~~ heading to. So they have to walk the rest of the
way. They stop at a pool of water to rest for the night before they got
to the new ranch.
Ranch-hands travel from ranch to ranch.
George makes Lennie give up a dead mouse he keeps in his pocket.
George throws it in the woods.

Characters in the book: Lennie and George

Setting

Plot

◁—◁

Lennie had the mouse in his pocket, he was petting it. He probably killed it by petting it too rough, even though he told George it was already dead.

✳ Mr. Blister says its important to remember that Lennie killed the mouse on accident —by loving it too much and petting its head until it bites him and then it gets killed, but not on purpose. Lennie is big, the mouse is small When George tells Lennie to get firewood, Lennie goes and gets the mouse back. George knows he went and got the mouse because Lenny only brings back one twig George throws the mouse even farther into the woods. 🌲🌲🌲

Lenny makes George tell him his favorite story about what they'll do once they get their stake. He tells him the story while they eat beans they cooked on the fire.

✳ stake — a good amount of money 💲💲💲 (also called jack)

bindle — a travelers pack with a sleeping bag and food and supplies. Hobos have them Most ranch-hands travel alone. That's what makes Lennie and George different from other ranch-hands.

Lennie likes Rabbits ————————→

Setting is a wooded stream or small lake near the ranch and the highway.

George talks mean to Lennie, but he really loves him. He just gets frustrated.

He makes Lennie remember to come back to this place if he ever gets in trouble. The George will come and find him. All Lennie has to do is come back to this place.

rug?

← Mr. Blister

See page 150 for Quick Quiz 5 answers.

Revision Tip #4:
Every Night, Review and Revise Notes for Two Classes

Review and revise your notes as often as possible. It's much easier to revise notes every day or two than it is to revise notes every week or two or just before tests. When you get too many notes to revise, it takes forever, plus it's hard to remember everything the teacher was talking about way back when, so it's harder to make headings.

So make it easy on yourself. Every night, revise the notes from two classes, whether you have a test or not. That way, your notes will always be neat and organized and you will be amazed by how much more stuff you remember.

"Beauregard, oh Beauregard!" called Babette. "I am finished."

Beauregard sauntered in.

"You reek!" said Babette.

"I'm sorry. The tuna fish smelled so good, I also kind of rolled in it. I don't know what came over me. I think I'm in love."

"Whatever. Beauregard, my revision work is done."

Beauregard looked over Babette's revised notes.

"Fabulous. You've done a wonderful job."

"And the best part is, by revising my notes, I already remember so much more about the book and about what we talked about in class.

"Exactly. By revising your notes, you already have a jump on studying for the test!"

"Okay, great," said Babette, "Now please leave. I must study."

"No problem," said Beauregard, and he waddled back to the living room where Brenda was sitting, eating tuna, and watching "Dawson's Creek."

"Do you like this show?" asked Beauregard.

"Meow," said Brenda, offering him a half-eaten can.

"Mmmm. Bumblebee tuna," groaned Beauregard. "In oil. I can't seem to get enough of it."

They sat and watched "Dawson's Creek" together. Beauregard inched closer to Brenda. She inched farther away. He thought it was because Brenda didn't like him, but it was really just because Beauregard smelled terrible. He needed a bath.

QUICK SUMMARY OF CHAPTER 4

★ Babette took notes in all her classes.

★ There are three important things you must do when taking notes in class:

  1. Be Neat.

  2. Listen Carefully.

  3. When the teacher changes the subject, draw a line in your notes.

★ Get the phone numbers of a couple friends in each class in case you have questions at night.

★ Babette was having trouble reading her notes on the book *Of Mice and Men*.

★ Beauregard gave her some tips on revising her notes.

★ Take notes on the left-hand page of your notebook.

★ Revise your notes on the right-hand page.

★ Make headings for different topics the teacher discussed.

★ Check off your notes on the left-hand page as you revise them on the right.

★ Underline, circle, and star the really important notes.

★ Revise the notes for two classes every night. Don't wait until you have a test or report due.

Chapter 5
Reading to Remember

WEDNESDAY

Meanwhile, back in Barnaby's apartment, Barnaby's parents had fallen asleep watching a television show about how to make a lot of money selling rotten tomatoes.

"By buying rotten tomatoes at rock-bottom prices, you, the consumer, are able to control your future," said a tanned man with black hair and white teeth. "To find out how, just send me, Steve Stevely, $19.95, and I'll send you all the information you need to control your future and become richer than you ever imagined!"

"Able to control your future," thought Barnaby, switching off the TV and covering his snoring parents with afghans. "Richer than I ever imagined. Now that would be cool. And all for $19.95."

Barnaby wandered into the kitchen and poured himself a glass of skim milk. As he was putting the milk back into the refrigerator, he noticed a reddish-brown substance in a sealed baggie in the vegetable drawer. He picked it up. The substance oozed to one corner of the baggie and kind of bubbled and gurgled.

He took a sip of milk.

"How could you control your future by buying a bunch of this rotten vegetable gunk?" wondered Barnaby. "If I sent Steve Stevely $19.95, I'd be totally broke, but I still want to find out. I guess this supergenius is on his own."

Barnaby took his glass of milk and the baggie full of rotten tomatoes into his bedroom and closed the door. He set each on his desk and pulled his laptop computer out of his hair. He plugged it into his phone and in a matter of minutes was surfing the Internet.

Computer Tip:
Study Help on the Internet

The internet is a great place to find out all sorts of stuff on whatever you are studying in school. All you need is a computer, a phone line, a modem or cable connection, and a computer program called an internet browser that allows you to get on the internet. Your school probably has computers hooked to the internet, and you may be able to get on-line yourself at home. Here are a few good websites for you to check out when you need help with your homework:

www.startribune.com/stonline/html/special/homework/

www.jiskha.com/

www.schoolwork.org/

chat.freezone.com/chatbox.html

www.upland.k12.ca.us/baldyvw/megaw.html

Barnaby did a search for articles on rotten tomatoes.

"*Fried Green Tomatoes, Attack of the Killer Tomatoes, 101 Healthy Tomato Recipes, Tomatoes vs. Potatoes—The Great Debate,*" Barnaby scrolled down the list of all titles that had to do with tomatoes until he found what he was looking for.

"Eureka!" he squeaked. "Thirty-two articles on 'Rotten Tomatoes and Your Future.'" He paused.

"Thirty-two articles?" he said to himself. "That's a lot of reading. I really don't have enough time to do all that reading."

Just then, Barnaby got an e-mail from Bridget.

To: Einstein@mellmanmiddleschool.edu (Barnaby)

From: ILuvIhop@grandson.com (Bridget)

Re: A Big Favor

Hey there Barnaby, Bridget here. Just wanted to let you know how things are going with the Grandson European tour. One word, Barnaby: Terrible! Thackeray has drummer's elbow, so we've had to rig up a computerized drum set that he controls by blinking his eyes. And Sailor is getting such a big head! Now he's demanding fresh Sunny Delight be shipped directly from the Sunny D factory every night so he can have *the freshest* Sunny Delight every morning to mix into his high-protein health shake. "Where's my fresh Sunny D? Where's my fresh Sunny D? This Sunny D isn't fresh enough! I need fresher Sunny D!" That's all I hear out of his little, itty-bitty, teeny-weeny mouth!

If it weren't for Ihop, I would have quit hours ago.

Ihop is so dreamy. He taught me a guitar chord this afternoon. I've been playing it for the last two hours on the guitar he loaned me. I call it "Ihop's chord." I really like Ihop. But he doesn't even know I exist. He's infatuated with some Olympic gymnast named Tara Trampolinski. I could just die.

But, anyway, the reason I'm writing is this: Barnaby, could you do me a big favor? The Grandson boys' grandfather Gus has been harassing me for news from the tour. He calls ten times a day. He wants to know how Grandson is being covered in the press. The problem is, Grandpa Gus is almost blind. He has to use this big magnifying glass and a flashlight to read the paper, so he gets tired fast.

What I'm asking you to do is this. I want to send you every Grandson concert review from their European tour. Could you and Babette and Beauregard go through and summarize these articles? That way, Grandpa Gus can read about all the concerts, but it won't take him as long, so he won't strain his eyes and get tired.

Grandpa Gus has been such a dear throughout the concert, I really wanted to do this for him myself, but I just don't have any time, as Babette may have told you (she helped me with my scheduling you know, such a dear friend that Babette).

Please, please do this for me Barnaby.

Thanks!

:) Bridget

Barnaby put aside his rotten tomato research for a moment and replied to Bridget.

To: ILuvIhop@grandson.com (Bridget)

From: Einstein@mellmanmiddleschool.edu (Barnaby)

Re: A Big Favor

The tour sounds awful! Not only do you have to listen to that terrible Grandson music every day, you are also slave to Sailor's Sunny D addiction. I feel for you Bridget, I really do. I think it's time for you to come back to Mellman—we miss you!

Babette, Beauregard, and I will definitely help you out by summarizing the Grandson articles for Grandpa Gus. Please, fax them all to me right away, and we'll get them back to you as soon as we can.

;) Barnaby

Bridget read Barnaby's e-mail with glee. She gathered together all the reviews and articles about the Grandson "Young As I Wanna Be" European tour and faxed them to Barnaby at his house. Barnaby's parents had a fax machine in their home office. Barnaby put his laptop back into his hair and tiptoed past his parents, who were still asleep under their afghans. He left for Babette's apartment, taking the pile of articles with him.

"BZZ BZZ," Babette's doorbell sounded.

"Who's there?" asked Babette.

"Me. Barnaby. Let me in."

"Why?"

"Bridget needs you and me to do her and Grandpa Gus a big favor."

"Grandpa who?" asked Babette.

"Just let me in!" squeaked Barnaby.

Babette let Barnaby into her apartment. "We need to write short summaries of some articles about Grandson so that Ihop, Thackeray, and Sailor's grandfather can read about their tour. I need your help."

"Well, Barnaby, I'll help you, but first I need you to do me a huge favor. I need you to give Beauregard a bath. He rolled around in tuna and he stinks. He's waiting for me in the bathroom, but I don't want to ruin my outfit by bathing him," Babette said, frustration knotting her voice.

"Yuck! Well, I guess I can help you out if you help me write the summaries," said Barnaby.

"It's a deal," said Babette.

Barnaby opened the bathroom door. There was Beauregard, looking as angry as Barnaby had ever seen him.

"What happened?" Barnaby ask Babette.

"He got a little overexcited with his tuna and ended up rolling in it like a dog."

"Why did he want to roll around in tuna?"

"Don't ask me."

"Do I look like a lamppost?" asked Beauregard.

"Uh, no," said Barnaby.

"Then why are you talking as if I'm not even here?"

"I just . . . um, I don't . . ., oh gosh, I'm sorry, Beauregard," said Barnaby. "You just don't look like you're much up for conversation at this moment."

"Why do you say that? Maybe because I was deprived of tuna for so long I went crazy when I finally got it, so I rolled in it. Is that why I look like I'm not up for conversation?"

"I'm sorry, Beauregard, but you've got to have a bath. Babette, you should step out of the bathroom. This could get ugly."

Babette left, closing the door behind her, but the horrible noises coming from the bathroom were as loud and clear as if she were still in there. Barnaby yelled. Beauregard screeched. The sound of water gushing made her think that a flood was about to start pouring out from under the door. A few minutes later Beauregard emerged soaking wet, but smelling clean. Then Barnaby appeared, one towel wrapped around his waist, another turban-style on his head. By the look on his face Babette could tell he was not happy.

"That cat is a monster," Barnaby said.

"I was manhandled by that mean supergenius!" Beauregard growled.

"Meow," said Brenda, relieved Beauregard didn't stink anymore.

"This is bad," said Babette.

Beauregard just hissed.

"I'm going to get dressed, so we can get down to work. Beauregard, don't you go anywhere. I need your help."

"What? You humans! You are all the same. You abuse and abuse and abuse and then have the gall to ask for help. Where do you get the nerve to ask me to help you with *anything?*"

By the time Beauregard finished ranting about the evil of humans, Barnaby had come out of the bathroom, dressed.

"If you help me, I'll give you thirty cans of tuna. Bumblebee tuna," Barnaby said.

"Packed in oil?"

"Yes, packed in oil."

"Can I eat as many cans at once as I want?"

"I suppose," said Barnaby. "Although your behavior does worry me a little bit."

"But, I just love Bumblebee tuna," said Barnaby. "It's a deal. Thirty cans. Now, what are we doing?"

"I have with me a stack of articles about Grandson's European tour. You, me, and Babette need to write short summaries of the articles so the Grandson boys' grandfather, Gus, can read about them. His eyes are getting bad and the articles are too long and the print is too small for him."

Barnaby took an article and handed Beauregard and Babette one article each. Babette got paper and pencils for everyone from her room, and they got down to work. Brenda sat close by and napped.

How to Take Notes on an Article or Textbook Tip

When you have a reading assignment, it's a good idea to read with a pencil in your hand. Why? Well, reading stuff for class is different than reading stuff for fun. When you're reading for fun, you remember the things you want to remember and forget the things you want to forget. It isn't important that you remember everything when you're reading a book, a magazine, or a newspaper for yourself. You're just reading for fun about something you like to read about. When you're reading for class, though, you have to remember the important stuff, and the best way to do that is by taking notes as you read.

Taking notes while you read is different from taking notes in class, because you already have all of the information written down. It's right there in the article or textbook you are reading. All you need to do now is mark the important stuff. There are three steps to taking good notes on reading material:

1. Read it once very carefully *without* a pencil.

2. Read it again *with* a pencil, marking key passages.

3. Write a *summary* of the article using the notes you took.

Let's take a closer look at those three steps.

1. Read it once very carefully without a pencil. Read the article through from start to finish. Read it like you'd read a good book or an article in your favorite magazine. Don't worry about remembering everything, just read it and pay attention.

2. Read it again with a pencil. Now read it again, but this time have a pencil ready. Take note of the important parts of the article. How do you know what the important parts are? That's a good question. While you are reading, ask yourself the following questions about what you are reading:

★ **Who** or **what** is the article about?

★ **When** did the things in the article happen?

★ **Where** did the things in the article happen?

★ **What*** is the article trying to say?

If what you are reading answers any of these questions, take note of the specific passage. If you can write in your book, underline the passage and write in the margin next to it: "Who," "When," "Where," or "What." These are the Four Ws. If you can't write in the book, copy key phrases into a notebook and follow the same instructions with the Four Ws.

You probably noticed that we listed one of the Ws—What—twice. That is because What has two different meanings here. One is "What is the subject of the article?" The other is "What is the article trying to say about the subject matter?" We put an asterisk (*) by the second What*. This What* is about the writer's opinion or an overall theme of the article. Sometimes when you read, the writer has no opinion. For example, a textbook writer usually doesn't have an opinion. She is just writing the facts. But some other writers do have opinions, so if a writer gives an opinion, like "This play is terrible" or "I love McDonald's french fries," or if you discover an overall theme to the article, underline that and write What*—with an asterisk (*)—in the margin beside it.

3. Write a summary of the article using the notes you took. Once you have read through the article and underlined or rewritten the important parts and written the four Ws in the margin, write a short summary of the article. A summary is a paragraph you write in your own words about the important parts of what you just read. Focus on the things you underlined when you write your summary. By writing a summary, you'll have an easier time remembering what you read when you take a quiz or a test on it.

After a few minutes, Barnaby was done with his first article. He looked to see how Babette and Beauregard were doing. Both looked confused.

"What's the matter guys?" asked Barnaby.

"Um, nothing," said Babette.

"Nothing at all," said Beauregard.

"It doesn't look like you're making too much progress on those articles."

"And you are?" asked Babette.

"Yes. I'm done with my first one."

"Oh. Well, let me see it," said Babette. "Just to make sure you're doing it the right way."

"Me, too," said Beauregard. "Just to make sure you're doing it the right way."

"See, that's exactly what I was going to do," said Beauregard. "I was going to underline the important stuff, write the Four

Ws out to the side, and then write a short summary based on the underlined stuff."

"Me, too," said Babette.

ARTICLE 1

The London Herald Times Tribune Gazette

Who **Grandson Proves Age Is Everything**

When **Grandson's August 31 Concert at Wembley Stadium**
Where by Quentin Tarantula

Youth. It has been wasted on Grandson.

In what was called the "concert of the decade," the pop group Grandson proved that a little talent and a lot of hype add up to a big waste of this reviewer's time.

What* authors opinion

You've heard of Grandson, no doubt. Their fresh faces have been plastered on enough buses, billboards, and boarded-up buildings to make this reviewer afraid to leave his house. The three young brothers, who cut their musical teeth in the malls and county fairs of Nebraska, USA, have taken England by storm. And a wicked storm it has been.

Where

After a successful appearance on the popular television show *Top of the Pops*, Grandson has played every concert hall in merry old England, from Leeds to Liverpool. This reviewer attended their benefit concert at Wembley Stadium. The concert raised money for crooked-toothed chimpanzees who cannot afford braces. With special guests like The Space Grrrls, Call Me Cute, and Sir Felton Jack slated to appear, tickets to the concert were being sold outside the stadium for more than £1,000. This reviewer would have gladly sold his ticket for a tenth of that price. But, alas, this reviewer did not.

What

What

Who

The concert began with the trio's number one smash hit, "Good Guy Groove." With Sailor's voice cracking on every third note, Ihop's guitar hopelessly out of tune, and Thackeray's drumming terribly offbeat, "Good Guy Groove" sounded "bad, bad, bad."

What

What* authors opinion

After steadily improving over the next few tunes ("Kim's Not My Type," "Hall Monitor," "Ring Around the Rosey"), Grandson welcomed The Space Grrrls onto the stage. Greeted with shouts of "Grrrl Power!" the five singers who make up The Space Grrrls joined in on Grandson's second biggest hit, "Fighting is for Fools."

What

What a disaster.

Outer Space kept falling to her left (later attributed by her publicist to a rare inner-ear infection). Gipper Space's outfit required electrical power as it was covered in high-voltage light bulbs, causing the rest of The Space Grrrls and Grandson to squint and turn away from her glaringly obvious attire. Thankfully, The Space Grrrls only sang one more song, "Frère Jacques," with Grandson before being led offstage by security guards.

Who

Who

Call Me Cute came on next. And this reviewer will! These adorable children from Iceland are about the cutest band members this reviewer has ever seen. Unfortunately, someone forgot to tell Call Me Cute that Grandson sings their songs in English, not Icelandic. What resulted was a horrifying duet, with Grandson singing the words to "Icicle Eyes" in English and Call Me Cute singing them in Icelandic.

Who

What

Who

This reviewer's ears are still ringing from that one.

Finally, Felton Jack came on to save the day. While his voice was in top form, his choice of outfits was quite disturbing: a purple double-breasted suit, yellow shoes, and a straw hat with a price tag hanging off the front. If somebody doesn't replace his dead personal designer, Kiki Krayola, soon, audiences will begin to cower from the image of Mr. Jack cranking out his hits live, on stage. This reviewer can promise you that.

Barnaby's Summary of the Article for Grandpa Gus

This article appeared in <u>The London Herald Times Tribune Gazette</u>. It's about a <u>Grandson</u> **(Who)** concert that took place on <u>August 31</u> **(When)** at <u>Wembley Stadium</u> **(Where)**. Quentin Tarantula wrote the article. Tarantula said the concert was a <u>big waste of his time</u> **(What*, author opinion)**. Grandson are three young brothers <u>from Nebraska</u> **(Where)**. They are:

1. <u>Sailor</u>

2. <u>Ihop</u>

3. <u>Thackeray</u> **(Who)**

They appeared on the television show <u>Top of the Pops</u> **(What)** and a bunch of concerts in England before playing this benefit concert at Wembley Stadium. The concert was <u>for poor chimpanzees with bad teeth</u> **(What)**. Grandson had three special guests:

1. The Space Grrrls

2. Call Me Cute

3. Sir Felton Jack **(Who)**

They played their big hit "<u>Good Guy Groove</u>." **(What)** Sailor, Ihop, and Thackeray <u>all sounded terrible</u>. **(What*/author opinion)** The Space Grrrls came on stage and sang with them. Outer Space kept falling over and Gipper Space wore a costume covered in lightbulbs. <u>Call Me Cute</u> **(Who)** followed them. They are from Iceland. They sang a bad duet with Grandson. <u>Felton Jack</u> **(Who)** came on last. He was dressed in a funny outfit. His designer, Kiki Krayola, is dead.

Big Mega-Important Summary Tip:
Make Lists When You Can

When Barnaby wrote his summary of the Grandson concert review, he used lists to help him remember the important names mentioned in the article. He listed the three special guests Grandson had at their concert:

1. The Space Grrrls

2. Call Me Cute

3. Sir Felton Jack

He also listed the names of the Grandson band members:

1. Ihop

2. Sailor

3. Thackeray

Whenever you can list things in your summary, do it! Lists make information easier for you to remember, and it makes your summaries easier to study from later.

"Looks good, Barnaby," said Babette. "Nice job."

"Yes, a fine job," agreed Beauregard. "Now, if you'll just leave us alone, maybe we can finish up our articles, too."

"Of course," said Barnaby. "So sorry to bother you."

"And don't forget," reminded Beauregard, "about all the tuna you promised me. Thirty cans."

"Of course I won't, Beauregard," replied Barnaby. "I am a supergenius and never forget a thing."

Beauregard got to work on his article, which had been written by an inmate at Liverpool Prison.

Quick Quiz 6

Take Notes on Beauregard's Article and Summarize It

Take notes on this article like Barnaby did, underlining important parts and writing the Four Ws (What, Who, Where, When) off to the side.

Article 2

The Prisoners' News
Grandson Does Good Time
Grandson's August 23rd Concert at Liverpool Prison

Yesterday's Grandson concert was the hottest show to hit the British Prison System since The Rolling Stones played the Thames Correctional Facility in 1979. I was there for that show, serving five to ten years for stealing Q-Tips from the London Hospital for the Ear, and I was at Liverpool Prison for last night's Grandson show. (I'm currently serving a life sentence for calling Prince Charles "Prince Curlicue.")

by
Inmate #45J6732F

The crowd was in high spirits as Grandson took the stage. Such fine looking young lads. Sailor won us over immediately when he asked, "How many of you think I'm pretty?" From there, Grandson launched into their international number-one smash hit "Good Guy Groove." Those boys sure were good players. Ihop's guitar crackled like the fire I set in the warden's office. Thackeray's drums burst like rotten tomatoes on a car's windshield. And Sailor's voice was as smooth as my lawyer is when she asks the judge why a nice guy like me, Inmate #45J6732F, has to stay in prison for so long for calling Prince Charles "Prince Curlicue."

I wasn't really paying attention for the rest of the show, but from the sound of the crowd, I bet it was really, really good.

Summarize the Article for Grandpa Gus Here

_____

_____

_____

_____

_____

_____

_____

_____

_____

_____

_____

_____

_____

_____

_____

_____

_____

See page 151 for Quick Quiz 6 answers.

Reassuring Summary Tip:
Like Snowflakes, No Two Summaries Are
Exactly Alike

Your summaries don't have to match Babette and Beauregard's summaries exactly. They just have to cover most of the same stuff—who played, where they played, any special stuff that happened at the concert, and what the writer thought about the concert and the band.

Babette was the last to finish reading and summarizing her article.

"What's taking you so long?" asked Barnaby.

"I am very thorough," she replied.

Quick Quiz 7

Take Notes on Babette's Article and Summarize It

Take notes on this article like Barnaby did on page 67, underlining important parts and writing the Four Ws (What, Who, Where, When) off to the side.

Article 3

Spun Magazine
Supermodels Love Grandson
by Johnny Lightning

August 25, Silver Dollar Arcade
Melbourne, Australia

Grandson's surprise concert at the Silver Dollar Arcade wasn't a surprise to the world's supermodels. Nobody, except for writers like me, was supposed to know that Grandson was playing a surprise show at this tiny video game arcade in Melbourne, Australia. Somehow, word got out, and before you knew it the Silver Dollar Arcade was transformed from a room full of kids and video games into a room full of supermodels and Arab sheiks.

Supermodel Claudia Shiftless arrived on the arm of Sheik Magic Salami; supermodel Tyra Tanks arrived on the arm of Sheik Vava Voom; and supermodel Courtney Dove arrived on the arm of Sheik I. Kiltcurt.

With all of the sheiks and supermodels, it was hard for me to focus on Grandson, who played their hit song "Good Guy Groove" quietly in the corner. I did notice that Sailor Grandson was more interested in the Mortal Kombat video game over by the wall than he was in singing, but Grandson sounded just fine, anyway.

After the show, I played against Sailor in Mortal Kombat, and he beat me in front of all those supermodels. They laughed at me for losing to a teenager. It was embarrassing.

Summarize the Article for Grandpa Gus Here

_____

_____

_____

_____

_____

_____

_____

_____

_____

_____

_____

_____

_____

_____

_____

_____

_____

_____

See page 153 for Quick Quiz 7 answers.

QUICK QUIZ 8 ON ALL THREE ARTICLES

You just did a Quick Quiz summarizing the articles Beauregard and Babette read and summarized. Now, go back and reread Barnaby's article and summary.

Did you do that? Okay, good. Now, reread the Babbette's and Beauregard's articles and summaries, and the story of how they came to write them. Now, take the following ten-question quiz on all three articles about the Grandson concerts. Don't look back at the articles when you take the test. Try to do it from memory, as if you were taking a test in class.

1. What cause did Grandson play a benefit concert for?

   A. Overeager beavers

   B. Crooked-toothed chimpanzees

   C. Three-legged sparrows

2. For what kind of people did Grandson play in the Silver Dollar Video Arcade?

   A. Supermodels and sheiks

   B. Librarians and pro wrestlers

   C. Movie stars and race car drivers

3. What did Inmate #45J6732F think of Prince Charles?

   A. He thinks Prince Charles is a nice guy.

   B. He thinks Prince Charles is a good golfer.

   C. He thinks Prince Charles has curlicue hair.

4. On what video game did one of the writers play Sailor?

   A. Mortal Kombat

   B. Donkey Kong

   C. Doom

5. The writer_____at the video game.

   A. beat Sailor

   B. tied Sailor

   C. lost to Sailor

6. Who is the guitarist for Grandson?

   A. Ihop

   B. Thackeray

   C. Sailor

7. What was the hit song Grandson played at each concert?

   A. Smells Like Teen Spirit

   B. Good Guy Groove

   C. Bang a Gong

8. Which of the following bands played with Grandson at a concert?

   A. Jerky Jeff and the Jeffmeisters

   B. The Rolling Stones

   C. The Space Grrls

9. What month did all three concerts get played in?

   A. July

   B. August

   C. September

10. Who did Barnaby, Babette, and Beauregard write their article summaries for?

   A. their English teacher

   B. R. L. Stine

   C. Grandpa Gus Grandson

See page 154 for Quick Quiz 8 answers.

Barnaby, Babette, and Beauregard summarized the rest of the articles for Grandpa Gus, about ten in all. When they were done, Barnaby reached in his hair and got a Federal Express overnight envelope. He put the article summaries in the Federal Express envelope so he could send them back to Bridget.

"That should help out good old Grandpa Gus a bunch," said Barnaby. "Now he won't have to read the whole article with his magnifying glass and a flashlight. Now Bridget owes me a big favor."

"And now I won't go hungry," said Beauregard.

"What?" asked Barnaby.

"You forgot! You vile human! You forgot about my thirty cans of tuna! And you call yourself a supergenius!"

"Relax, Beauregard," said Babette. "You are so excitable these days. You will get your tuna. Won't he, Barnaby?"

"Of course."

"Well," said Beauregard. "I'm waiting."

"Uh, Babette, got any money?" asked Barnaby.

"No," said Babette. "And I'm tired anyway. I have to go to sleep. Please leave."

Beauregard glared at Barnaby, his eyes revealing the anger that only a cat who doesn't have his thirty cans of tuna can feel.

"Meow," said Brenda.

"Can you wait until morning, Beauregard?" asked Barnaby. "I just need to make a few calls, plus it's late and all."

"Fine. I'll give you until breakfast tomorrow morning. If I don't get my tuna by breakfast, you will be very, very sorry."

QUICK SUMMARY OF CHAPTER 5

★ Barnaby was surfing the internet for articles about rotten tomatoes.

★ While he was on the internet, he got an e-mail from Bridget.

★ She needed help summarizing Grandson concert reviews for Grandson's grandfather, Grandpa Gus.

★ Barnaby convinced Beauregard and Babette to help him summarize the articles. He promised Beauregard thirty cans of tuna for his help.

★ The first step of summarizing articles is to underline or rewrite the important parts of the article that have to do with the Four Ws:

1. What
2. Who
3. When
4. Where

★ The "What" has two parts: *what* the article is about, and *what* the author thinks. If the author is not expressing an opinion on the subject, you don't have to worry about the second "What."

★ Barnaby marked up and summarized the first article. Babette and Beauregard then did the same thing with their articles.

★ Barnaby sent the articles back overnight to Bridget. Now Bridget owes Barnaby a big favor.

Chapter 6
Study Techniques

Barnaby stayed up late into the night, thinking of ways to get Beauregard his thirty cans of tuna. It was not smart to get Beauregard mad. Beauregard had certain friends in low places who could make the life of a supergenius very dangerous.

But all Barnaby had to his name was $11, and there was no way $11 was going to buy thirty cans of tuna. Ever since Bumblebee had gone "dolphin-safe," the prices had skyrocketed. Barnaby checked his parents' cupboards—two cans of tuna, and it wasn't Bumblebee, and it was packed in spring water, not oil. If there was anything that made Beauregard madder than not having tuna, it was having tuna packed in spring water.

Barnaby called Babette, but her answering machine picked up, and Barnaby knew if he left a message, Beauregard would hear it, and then he would really be in big trouble. Barnaby got his laptop out of his hair and plugged it into the phone jack in his kitchen. He logged on to the internet to see if there were any discount stores in the area that could deliver thirty cans of Bumblebee tuna by breakfast time. Of course, there were no such places. Barnaby fell asleep in the kitchen and had terrible dreams.

When Barnaby woke in the morning, the keyboard had left an imprint on his left cheek. His mother came from the living room, where she'd slept all night on the couch under an afghan. She was startled to see her son.

"Barnaby!" exclaimed his mom. "What on earth happened to you?"

"Oh, sorry," said Barnaby. "I fell asleep here last night while I was on the internet. I guess I slept all night on my computer keyboard."

"Your dad and I fell asleep on the couches last night. I guess nobody wanted to sleep on their beds last night for some reason."

"Yeah, for some reason." said Barnaby.

"Are you okay? You look worried."

"Oh, no, it's nothing. Um, are those the only cans of tuna we have, the Chicken of the Sea packed in spring water?"

"Yes. Why?"

"Oh, nothing. Science project. For my students," said Barnaby. "Um, can I borrow $20?"

"No, sorry son, cash is a little tight right now," said Barnaby's mother and quickly left the kitchen.

The phone rang. Barnaby's mom was in the shower. Barnaby's dad had already left for work (billboard painters get a very early start). Barnaby picked up the phone.

"Hello?"

"Meow," said Brenda.

"Oh, good, it's just you."

"And me," said Beauregard.

"Oh, hi Beauregard, and how are you this morning? Have a good night's sleep I hope?"

"Oh, I slept like a baby," said Beauregard, "Because I knew when I woke up, I would have thirty cans of Bumblebee tuna, packed in oil, for me to eat, roll in, and do whatever I wanted with."

"Yes, yes, of course. No wonder you slept so well."

"So. When can I expect you? And the tuna?"

"Um, see, Beauregard, Mr. Beauregard sir, I'm having a little trouble coming up with thirty cans right this moment, but I'm working on it."

"That is too bad," said Beauregard, "for you."

"I could get you eleven cans, but the other nineteen cans are going to take a little longer."

"How much longer?"

"Tomorrow?"

"Tomorrow! You lowly humans, making your promises, then breaking them, over and over again. I tell you what, Barnaby, I'm going to give you until tomorrow, but you will have to pay interest on those cans of tuna."

"How much?" said Barnaby, stinging from the mention of interest.

"One hundred percent! That's right—tomorrow morning, you owe me thirty more cans of tuna! Making the total sixty cans!"

"Sixty cans! I can't come up with sixty cans of Bumblebee tuna by tomorrow morning! That's impossible! I have classes to teach today! I can't get you sixty cans!"

"Then you will pay in other ways."

"Okay. I'm sorry. Yes sir, Mr. Beauregard. Sixty cans it is."

"I'll send some of my people over to collect the eleven cans you have. Good day."

Beauregard hung up the phone. Barnaby got dressed fast and ran to the grocery store with his $11 and bought eleven cans of Bumblebee tuna in oil. When he got back to his apartment, Beauregard's goons were waiting for him.

"You Barnaby?" asked one of them, a huge cat with claws like box cutters and teeth like a tiger's.

"Who wants to know?" asked Barnaby.

"Me. That's who," said the other goon, an even bigger cat with claws like switchblades and teeth like elephant tusks.

"Yes, yes, I'm Barnaby. I suppose you're here for these."

Barnaby handed the first cat the grocery bag. The scary cat with box-cutter claws counted the cans.

"They're all here," said the cat to his bigger friend. "Mr. B says we will be picking up forty-nine more of these tomorrow, making the total number of cans sixty. Same time, same place."

"Yes, yes, of course, forty-nine more tomorrow morning, right here, making the total number sixty."

"And no spring water!" yelled the big one with elephant-tusk teeth.

"Of course not, no spring water, tuna packed in oil, Bumblebee packed in oil."

"You're a smart kid," said the big one. "A supergenius, we've heard. Good looking, too. Make sure you don't mess this up, okay?"

"Of course not. I'll see you tomorrow."

The scary goon cats left. Barnaby closed the door to his apartment and flopped on the couch. He covered himself with his mother's afghan.

"What am I going to do?" he said to himself. "There is only one person I know who could help me get that much tuna on such short notice."

Barnaby got his laptop computer out of his hair and typed Bridget a frantic e-mail.

To: ILuvIhop@grandson.com (Bridget)

From: Einstein@mellmanmiddleschool.edu (Barnaby)

Subject: Urgent request for aid

Bridget, remember how you owe me a big favor for all those summaries Babette, Beauregard, and I wrote for Grandpa Gus? Well, I need that big favor sooner than I expected. I need it now. Here is my request:

I need to put on a benefit concert. The cause? My good health. See, I owe Beauregard more tuna than I can afford, and my parents can't help me.

I'd ask you or Babette for a small loan, but I need a LOT of money—more than $50. If I don't get Beauregard the Bumblebee tuna I owe him, I'm scared of what his goons are going to do to me. They are scary, his goons. Real scary. So, I was thinking that for this benefit concert, we could charge one can of tuna for admission.

I know Grandson is in the middle of their tour. I'm not asking you to send them over. What I am asking is for Felton Jack to come over. I know he just played a concert with Grandson—I read the article about it for Grandpa Gus. I also know that Mr. Jack isn't getting as many requests to play as he used to get (due to his newly pathetic fashion sense), so I'm hoping he might be eager to play for an audience—any audience.

Could you put a good word in for me with Mr. Jack? Could he come tonight on Grandson's private jet? I could book the gym at the middle school, put posters up advertising the concert, get him a backup band, the whole deal. I just need him TONIGHT.

Please get back to me as soon as you can, otherwise, I'm a little frightened of the consequences.

Desperately yours,
Barnaby

Barnaby sent the e-mail and went to the kitchen. He poured himself a glass of skim milk and drank it down. His stomach was churning. He was very nervous. If Felton Jack couldn't come, he was doomed. Barnaby paced around his house, folding afghans, straightening out the magazine pile, dusting. Finally, his computer beeped and he hoped it was Bridget sending him an e-mail back.

From: ILuvIhop@grandson.com
To: Einstein@mellmanmiddleschool.edu
Subject: Re: Urgent request for aid

What is Beauregard's deal? He is getting so sensitive and mean.

Anyway, Barnaby, you are one lucky supergenius. I just happen to have Felton Jack in my office right now! He said he will play your Bumblebee Benefit tonight, but he has three demands:

1. He needs backup singers who know all the words to "Bad Alligator," "Rocket Rock," and "Sharon's Song."

2. He needs a plate full of sandwiches, preferably bologna and mustard.

3. He needs a new outfit.

(Barnaby, I added that one. Felton is wearing a bright orange suit with blue shoes and a black policeman's cap. He needs serious fashion help.)

So Felton is on the way! The jet arrives at Kennedy Airport at 5:00 this evening. I will have the Grandson stretch limousine pick you up so you can go pick him up. Please be there to meet him.

And thank you for the article summaries for Grandpa Gus. They are great, and he will really appreciate them.

Good luck!

Bridget

Barnaby e-mailed Babette next.

To: Frenchbabe@mindspring.com (Babette)

From: Einstein@mellmanmiddleschool.edu (Barnaby)

Subject: Felton Jack is coming

Babette, big news! Felton Jack is coming to play tonight at the gymnasium! Much to do, can't talk now. Please come right over. We've got a lot of work to do. Don't worry about school. I am calling in now to arrange a substitute teacher to take over my classes. I will tell Principal Skinner that you are helping me with the Felton Jack benefit, so you won't get in any trouble.

You need to bring:

1. Words to Felton Jack's "Bad Alligator," "Rocket Rock," and "Sharon's Song."

2. Sewing materials and a lot of fabric. We need to make Mr. Jack a new outfit.

Come now!

Barnaby

Babette's alarm clock radio blared "Raging Randy's Morning Show." Babette woke and shuffled to her kitchen. She poured herself a glass of orange juice. There was a fishy smell coming from the living room.

"What could that be?" she wondered, her eyes still half-closed.

She sat down at her computer and logged into her e-mail account. She read the first sentence of Barnaby's e-mail message.

Babette, big news. Felton Jack is coming to play tonight at the gymnasium!

Babette spit her orange juice all over the keyboard. She ran back to the kitchen and got a dish towel. She wiped off her computer and read on.

"I don't believe it," she said out loud. "I'm going to meet Felton Jack! And I get to clothe him! Just like in my dream! This is my big chance!"

She ran to her bedroom and rummaged around in the bottom drawer of her dresser, where she kept all of her Felton Jack memorabilia. She found what she was looking for—her *Felton Jack Plays the Hits* songbook.

She closed the drawer and opened the one above it, the drawer with all of her personal sewing and fashion accessories. She fished out *Rock Star Patterns*, *How to Sew Clothes for the Big-Boned Person*, and *Mending for Dummies*. She stuffed them in her backpack with the songbook. She ran to the kitchen and got a big black plastic bag. She stuffed it full of fabric and thread and needles and buttons and zippers and everything she would need to clothe Felton Jack.

Babette showered, dressed, and was almost out the door on her way to Barnaby's place.

"See you later, Beauregard," she called into the living room. "I've got to go help Barnaby with some important work. Please clean up whatever you spilled in there. It smells terrible."

"Will do," said Beauregard.

"Meow," said Brenda.

"Well, well, well," said Beauregard to Brenda. "It looks like my intimidating friends got the supergenius off his duff."

"Meow," said Brenda.

"Please pass me another can of that fine Bumblebee tuna," he requested. "And open one for yourself, of course, my dear Brenda. This time tomorrow, we will be swimming in it."

Barnaby let Babette into his apartment.

"This is so exciting, Barnaby! How did you get Felton Jack? And what is the benefit concert for?"

"It is exciting. Bridget owed me a favor, so she got me Felton Jack. The benefit concert is for me."

"For you?" said Babette, surprised.

"It's a long story. Let's just say that if I don't have sixty cans of Bumblebee tuna by tomorrow morning, I'm in big trouble."

"I smell a rat."

"Yeah, more like a big talking cat."

"I do not understand what has gotten into Beauregard," said Babette. "Ever since he started hanging around with Brenda, he's been getting meaner and meaner."

"It must be love," said Barnaby, sarcastically. "But enough small talk. We don't have much time. I have made a schedule of what we need to do today."

"I remember schedules."

"Good, good. Here is one for you, and here is one for me."

Quick Quiz 9

Below are the activities that Barnaby and Babette need to do in preparation for the benefit concert. On the blank schedule provided, arrange the activities in a logical order, then check your schedule against the actual schedule to get an idea of how good you are at organizing your time.

Barnaby's Activities

Buy lots of bologna, white bread, and mustard (2 hours). Prepare Babette for the "Raging Randy" show (1 hour). Bumblebee Benefit Concert (2 hours). Assemble the school band for song practice (2 hours). Tape Posters all over town (2 hours). Pick up Felton Jack at the airport (1 hour). Make posters (1 hour). Go to A&P and buy Bumblebee tuna before store closes (1 hour). Put up the stage in the gym (1 hour).

Babette's Activities

Drive Felton Jack back to the airport (1 hour). Appear on the "Raging Randy" morning show to promote the concert (1 hour). Memorize words to three songs (1 hour). Bumblebee Benefit Concert (2 hours). Pick up Felton Jack at the airport (1 hour). Rehearse songs with the school band (2 hours). Call Bridget for Felton Jack's measurements (1 hour). Create clothes for Felton Jack (3 hours). Prepare for appearance on "Raging Randy" morning show (1 hour).

See page 155 for Quick Quiz 9 answers.

Name:	Date:
Time of Day	
6 a.m.	
7 a.m.	
8 a.m.	
9 a.m.	
10 a.m.	
11 a.m.	
noon	
1 p.m.	
2 p.m.	
3 p.m.	
4 p.m.	
5 p.m.	
6 p.m.	
7 p.m.	
8 p.m.	
9 p.m.	
10 p.m.	
11 p.m.	
midnight	

Name: **Date:**

Time of Day	
6 a.m.	
7 a.m.	
8 a.m.	
9 a.m.	
10 a.m.	
11 a.m.	
noon	
1 p.m.	
2 p.m.	
3 p.m.	
4 p.m.	
5 p.m.	
6 p.m.	
7 p.m.	
8 p.m.	
9 p.m.	
10 p.m.	
11 p.m.	
midnight	

"I have to go on the 'Raging Randy' show?" asked Babette.

"He has the most popular radio program in the city. I called him right after I e-mailed you, and he said someone could come on his show and talk about the concert. It will be good publicity."

"I see you want me to do the talking," said Babette, a little frightened. "I get very nervous in front of crowds you know. Plus I am French. Sometimes when I am nervous, I forget my English words."

"There will be no crowd," explained Barnaby. "Just you and Raging Randy."

"But there will be crowds and crowds of people listening, no?"

"Yes, there will. But Raging Randy will make you feel very comfortable. Don't worry."

"I will trust you this time, Barnaby, because I want this concert to be a success for you and for me. I will not forget my English words. I promise."

"Wait. What do you mean 'a success for me'?" asked Barnaby.

"I will be designing Mr. Felton Jack the outfit he will be wearing on stage. It will be my big chance to impress him now, so that after I go to Fashion High, he will surely remember me, and make me his personal fashion designer like he said he would in my dream."

"Oh yeah," said Barnaby. "I forgot about that. But enough chit chat. Let's get to work. I have to prepare you for the 'Raging Randy' show."

"Okay. Tell me what to say."

"You need to tell them he is taking Grandson's private jet straight from London's Heathrow Airport to play the concert. You need to tell them he will be playing his hit songs 'Bad Alligator,' 'Rocket Rock,' and 'Sharon's Song.' You need to tell them the concert will be starting at 6 p.m. You need to tell them it will be at the Mellman Middle School Gymnasium. You need to tell them that admission is one can of Bumblebee tuna, packed in oil, *not* water."

Babette looked at Barnaby.

"Got it?" asked Barnaby.

"*Non. C'est impossible!*" cried Babette.

"Uh oh, you're getting nervous aren't you?" asked Barnaby. "You're forgetting your English."

"I am sorry Barnaby," said Babette. "That is a lot of information. How will I ever remember to tell Raging Randy all of those things?"

"Hmm, good question. Sometimes I forget that everyone isn't a supergenius like me."

Barnaby fell deep into thought.

"I've got it!" he yelled "Flashcards!"

Barnaby reached into his hair and produced a pack of four-by-six-inch index cards.

Flashcard Tip:

You've probably used flashcards at some point in school. They are one of the best ways to memorize the definitions of words. They are also good ways to remember other, more complicated things, too. For any situation, flashcards are an excellent study tool.

Making a flashcard is easy. You can buy three-by-five- or four-by-six-inch index cards, or you can just cut a piece of notebook paper into four pieces. Then on one side you write the word, name, or problem. On the other side, you write the answer or the definition. Now you have a flashcard. So, if you have a quiz on the capitals of the fifty states, you can write Indiana on the front of the flashcard and Indianapolis on the back. If you have a quiz on multiplication tables, you can write "6 x 7 =" on one side, and "42" on the back.

"All you've got do is make a flashcard for each of the points you have to cover when you're on 'Raging Randy.' Here's a pencil."

Barnaby handed her a pencil and went through the things she had to remember on the "Raging Randy" radio show.

"Number one: Felton Jack is flying into New York from London today."

"How do I make a flashcard for that?" asked Babette.

"Simple. Make that statement into a question and an answer. Here, let me do the first one."

Barnaby wrote down the following on Babette's index card:

Q: Where is Felton Jack flying in from today?

A: London, England

"I get it," said Babette. "So I will make a question-and-answer flashcard for each of the things I need to remember for the 'Raging Randy' show. Go ahead, read them to me."

Flashcard Quick Quiz 10

Help Babette make her flashcards for the Raging Randy show. Following are the four other things Barnaby told her she needs to remember. Turn them into question-and-answer flashcards.

1. Felton Jack will be playing his hit songs "Bad Alligator," "Rocket Rock," and "Sharon's Song."

Front

Back

2. The concert will be starting at 6 p.m.

Front

Back

3.   It will be held at the Mellman Middle School Gymnasium.

Front

Back

4.   Admission price is one can of Bumblebee tuna, packed in oil, *not* water.

Front

| |
| |

Back

| |

See page 157 for Quick Quiz 10 answers.

Babette finished up her question-and-answer flashcards. Barnaby gave them a quick look.

"These are great, Babette," he said. "Now go catch a cab and study these on the way to the show. By the time you get there, you should have the information down, no problem. We are in business!"

"Could we study together first?" asked Babette.

"I don't have much time, but sure, for a few minutes."

Barnaby read her the questions from her question-and-answer flashcards.

Flashcard Tip:
Study with a Friend or Relative

Studying alone is important. But when you study with somebody else—a friend, your mom, your brother or sister—you learn by speaking and hearing, too. When you've actually said facts aloud and heard others say them to you, they're easier to remember. It's just how the brain works. If you have read through this book to this point, you probably realize that we're trying to get you to be actively involved in studying, instead of just reading the book and listening in class. We want you to use all of your brain, not just part of it.

"What is the price of admission?"

"One can of Bumblebee tuna, packed in oil, *not* water," answered Babette.

"What hit songs will Felton Jack be playing?

"Felton Jack will be playing 'Bad Alligator,' 'Rocket Rock,' and . . . and," Babette thought for a moment, "and 'Sharon's Song'!"

"That's right! You've got these down already!"

"Just *making* the flashcards made it easier for me to remember."

"That's called 'active studying,' Babette. It's what I teach my students. You learn better by doing. It's just how the human brain works."

"I like to learn by doing. This is fun! I could even learn math this way. Just read me the other three, and I will go catch my cab," said Babette.

Barnaby finished quizzing Babette, and Babette left with her flashcards.

"Good luck," said Barnaby. "While you're gone, I'll be making up the posters for the show."

Flashcard Tip:
The *FIVE* Ws

Remember the Four Ws from the last chapter on taking notes—"Who, What, When, and Where"? Well, you can use those same questions—plus you can add another W,—"Why"—to help you make really useful flashcards. You can make a question and answer out of a sentence by reconstructing the sentence using one, or sometimes more than one, of the Five Ws.

Here's an example:

Sentence

The Declaration of Independence was signed in 1776 in Philadelphia.

Question-and-Answer Flashcard

Q: When was the Declaration of Independence signed?

A: 1776

Here's another question-and-answer flashcard from this sentence:

Question-and-Answer Flashcard

   Q: Where was the Declaration of Independence signed?

   A: Philadelphia.

Once again, the Ws are really important when you study. To be a good reader, a good note-taker, and a good flashcard-maker, you *always* need to be asking yourself "Who, What, When, Where, and Why." By asking these questions, you aren't just memorizing some-thing—you are actually *learning* it. You will understand it. And you will remember it when test time rolls around.

Barnaby rummaged around in his hair until he had everything he needed for his posters: a notebook, a big piece of paper, a pencil, and some markers. He laid his paper out on the coffee table in the living room and got to work.

"Okay," he said to himself. "The first thing I've got to do is list the things I need to say on this poster."

Barnaby talked to himself when there was nobody around. He thought it was one of the keys to being a supergenius.

Here are the facts Barnaby noted for the poster:

★Poster title: Barnaby's Bumblebee Benefit Concert

★When: Tonight, September 1

★When: 6 p.m.

★Where: Mellman Middle School

   235 West 15th Street, New York City

★Price: Admission is one can of Bumblebee tuna, packed in oil, *not* water. Those who bring Bumblebee packed in water will not be allowed in.

★Who is playing: International pop star Felton Jack

★What will he be playing: All of his greatest hits, including "Bad Alligator," "Rocket Rock," and "Sharon's Song."

★Why he is playing: The concert is a benefit for Barnaby, who needs sixty cans of tuna or he is in big trouble.

"Okay," Barnaby said to himself. "That should about cover it. Now I'll sketch the poster in pencil and write the information in pencil, too."

So Barnaby sat down and sketched his poster in pencil so if he made a mistake, he could change it.

"Now I'll go over it with my markers and I will have one cool poster to put all over town."

This is what Barnaby came up with:

Barnaby's Bumblebee Benefit Concert
Featuring International Pop Star
Felton Jack
Playing all of his greatest Hits:
Bad Alligator, Rocket Rock and Sharon's Song

Concert is tonight, September 1
Starts at 6:00
Where: Mellman Middle School
235 West 15th Street, New York City

Admission is one can of Bumblebee tuna, packed in oil, not water.
Those who bring Bumblebee packed in water will not be allowed in.

Arts and Crafts Tip:
Making a Study Poster

You may have thought we were going on and on about Barnaby making his concert poster for absolutely no reason. Wrong! It was a trick! And you fell for it!

See, you can make a poster of the things you are studying in school. It's a great way to learn by doing. Plus, if you're good, it's an excellent wall decoration for your room.

Let's say, for example, that you are having a quiz about what Abraham Lincoln did when he was president of the United States. Here's how to make a study poster:

Step 1: Get Materials

★Class notebook

★Poster-size paper

★Pencil

★Colored Markers

Step 2: Make a List

In your social studies notebook, make a list of the facts you need to know about Abraham Lincoln when he was president.

★Abraham Lincoln served as president from 1861–1865

★He was president when the Union won the Civil War

★He gave the Gettysburg address in 1863

★He wrote the Emancipation Proclamation, which freed the slaves, in 1863

★He was assassinated by John Wilkes Booth in 1865

Step 3: Sketch the Main Idea of the Poster

Now get out your poster paper. Use your pencil for now. You can go back and color things in later.

Write the title of the poster in really big letters on top.

WHAT   ABRAHAM   LINCOLN   DID   WHEN
HE WAS PRESIDENT

Now draw a picture, with your pencil, of Mr. Lincoln doing one of the things you listed. Draw a picture of whatever you think is most important, for example, writing the Emancipation Proclamation. (Leave space around your picture for more writing and pictures.)

Now, below, or on top of the picture, write a caption for what you've just drawn:

Lincoln wrote the Emancipation Proclamation, which freed the slaves.

Step 4: Sketch the Rest of the Poster

After you've drawn and written the main idea, draw smaller pictures around the bigger one, and write the sentences that go with them. If you're not the best artist on the planet, you can just write down the other things from your notebook in the poster margins. But drawing pictures to go with them will help.

Step 5: Color It In

Get the colored markers and make your poster a work of art!

Step 6: Hang It on Your Bedroom Wall

Hang your gorgeous piece of study art on the wall where you can look at it. Read it whenever you can—at least five times before your test.

Barnaby took a look at his schedule.

"Now I have to make copies of the posters at the copy shop, and then I have the next two hours to plaster them all over town."

He flipped the radio on to the "Raging Randy" morning show.

"So *Babette!*" screamed Raging Randy. "*Have* a *boyfriend?*"

"I don't see what that has to do with the Felton Jack concert Mr. Randy," replied Babette.

"*Call* me *Raging!*" he yelled.

"No, thank you," said Babette. "As I was saying, Felton Jack will be playing 'Bad Alligator,' 'Rocket Rock,' and 'Sharon's Song.' The price of admission is one can of Bumblebee tuna, packed in oil. Make sure it is packed in oil, not water, or you will not be admitted."

"You *really know* your *stuff, Babette!*" yelled Raging Randy.

"Thank you, Mr. Randy. Now I must go."

"You don't want to hang around for the rest of the show?" screamed Raging Randy.

"No. I am sorry. I have a schedule to stick to. Hope to see everyone out there at the concert!"

With that Babette excused herself and caught a cab back to her apartment.

In the cab, she looked at her schedule.

"Next, I need to make Felton Jack a fashionable outfit."

She got home and e-mailed Bridget for Felton Jack's measurements. Bridget e-mailed her right back.

To: Frenchbabe@mindspring.com (Babette)

From: ILuvIhop@grandson.com (Bridget)

Subject   Felton Jack's girth

Felton Jack's measurements are as follows:

Waist: 48

Length: 28

Shoulder: 36

Arm: 32

Neck: 22

I know, not pretty, but do what you can. Thanks! See you soon, and best of luck with the concert. Rock on!

:) Bridget

Babette opened her backpack and got out her sewing books. She got out her fabric, her buttons, and her zippers. She got out her thread and her needles and her tape measure.

She started to read the directions for the outfit she had dreamed of creating for Felton Jack:

Outfits for the Big-Boned Rock Star

Creating an outfit for the big-boned rock star can be quite a challenge. The most important thing to remember is that you cannot make this person look skinny, no matter how hard you try.

That's about all the directions Babette read before she was cutting away at the red velvet fabric she had picked out.

A half-hour later, Barnaby showed up, home early from taping posters around town.

"Posters are up," said Barnaby. "With your great performance on Raging Randy's, and all the posters I put up today, we are assured of a huge turnout at the gymnasium tonight."

"Great!" said Babette. "And I am about halfway done with Mr. Jack's new red velvet jumpsuit."

She held it up and the both let out gasps of pure horror.

"*Mon dieu!*" screamed Babette. "What have I done?"

The Following Directions Tip:

Life is much easier if you follow directions. We aren't telling you that you shouldn't think for yourself. Following directions doesn't mean you should never question anything. But who do you want to be: somebody who drives around all day trying to find The World's Largest Ball of Twine by yourself and never does, or someone who pulls over when he is lost, asks directions, and actually gets to see the big ol' twine ball?

"That looks like it wouldn't fit a ten-year-old, much less a three-hundred-pound rock star with a weakness for bologna on white bread," scolded Barnaby. "What kind of fashion book are you reading?"

"Well, I did not really read it all very carefully," admitted Babette. "Actually, I did not read the directions *at all*. Perhaps I should take a closer look."

This time she read the directions carefully and found out where she had gone wrong. She had forgotten to take into account Felton Jack's "problem areas," particularly his stomach.

"And that was the last of my fabric!" cried Babette. "We are doomed!"

"Not yet, we aren't," said Barnaby. "If I don't get those sixty cans of Bumblebee tuna, I am doomed. What about using my parents afghans instead of the red velvet?"

"But they have had those afghans since 1979!" exclaimed Babette.

"Then it's time for them to get new ones. Come on! Use them! I'll explain to my parents later. But please, read the directions first this time."

"I promise I will," said Babette, and she did.

Outfits for the Big-Boned Rock Star

Creating an outfit for the big-boned rock star can be quite a challenge. The most important thing to remember is that you cannot make this person look skinny, no matter how hard you try.

The first step is cleaning your sewing needles. You need the cleanest of needles to be able to make many, many stitches in order to keep the seams from breaking when the rock star belts out those high notes.

The second step is buying stretchy fabric. An over-weight rock star cannot wear vinyl pants. He cannot wear a velvet V-neck shirt. Go with fabric that has Lycra in it, or elastic in it, or even rubber.

The third step is to use heavy-duty buttons and zippers. The buttons and zippers will be put through a lot of strain and stress, so it is important that they be the strongest, most reliable buttons and zippers you can find.

Barnaby gathered up his parents' afghans and put the pile in front of Babette.

"Thanks, Barnaby, these will work out great—they look really stretchy."

"No problem," said Barnaby. "Hey, um, Babette. You know what's next on my schedule?"

"No."

"Buying bologna, bread, and mustard."

"And?"

"And well, you know, I guess I have to buy these things and, well . . ." Barnaby trailed off.

"Oh. I forgot. You have no money and are afraid to ask for it. I tell you what. Here is ten dollars. You can pay me back whenever you can. No rush."

"Thank you Babette. I get my paycheck next Friday. I promise I'll pay you back then."

"Actually, Barnaby, you are saving me money by giving me these afghans, so I tell you what, we are even."

"Really?"

"Yes. Really. Go get your bologna. I have clothes to make!"

"Great. But don't forget about memorizing the songs. You have to sing backup for Felton tonight."

"That is no problem. Now get going!"

Babette followed the directions this time and made a fabulous jumpsuit for Felton. Then she got out her songbook.

Babette tried over and over to memorize the lyrics to Felton Jack's song, but they just weren't sticking in her mind. "I cannot remember anything!" cried Babette in frustration. Just then, Barnaby called.

"I'm at my wit's end," said Babette. "I am having a lot of trouble memorizing the words for 'Bad Alligator.'"

"What do I hear in the background?" asked Barnaby.

"Oh, just the radio and the television and—wait, I've got a call on the other line."

"Hello?" Babette asked after she clicked over to the other call

"Barnaby?" said his mother.

"No, I am sorry, this is his friend Babette."

"Oh, well, is Barnaby there?"

"No, he is on the other line actually."

"Well, tell him I have seen his posters around town, and he has got a *lot* of explaining to do!"

"I will tell him! Bye!"

"Who was that?" asked Barnaby.

"Your mother."

"Oh no. Well, right now, that is the least of my worries. Babette, you have to remove all distractions if you are to memorize those lyrics! Turn off the TV. Turn off the radio. Unplug the phone. You can't learn anything with all those other things going on around you."

"Okay. I will. Thank you, Barnaby.

"Wait! And meet me at school at 3 p.m. to rehearse the songs with the band."

"I will! Bye bye!"

Good Study Environment Tip:

To study well, you need to get rid of all distractions. Make a list of everything that stops you from studying, such as the TV, the radio, phone calls, noisy siblings. Go ahead and do it now.

_____   _____

_____   _____

_____   _____

_____   _____

_____   _____

Try to seclude yourself from the things on your list every time you study! Lock the door, unplug your phone, and definitely leave the television off. Studying in front of the TV is the easiest way to waste all of your good study habits.

The next thing you need to do is make a list of everything that helps you study. Some munchies, an open window, a picture of a hero of yours—anything that will keep you in that chair for as long as you need to be in that chair! Write those things in the space provided below.

_____	_____
_____	_____
_____	_____
_____	_____
_____	_____
_____	_____

Every time you study, look at your two lists: your study stoppers and your study helpers. Get rid of the things that hurt your studying and surround yourself with the things that help you study. Do this every single time you study.

Babette turned off the TV and the radio. She turned off the ringer on the phone. She went to Barnaby's refrigerator and got herself a glass of water and a piece of cheese. She sat down at a desk, and got down to work. In twenty minutes, she had the three songs memorized from beginning to end by employing active learning techniques.

She packed Felton Jack's outfit into her backpack and caught a cab to Mellman Middle School. The concert was a few short hours away!

Barnaby greeted her at the door.

"Babette! Just in time. Doesn't the band sound wonderful?"

"Yes!" agreed Babette, hopping on stage to practice the back-up lyrics with them. She had just enough time to go over each song before the Grandson limousine, which Bridget had sent for them, arrived to whisk them to the airport to meet Felton Jack.

In the limo Babette got her afghan creation out of her backpack, "Let me show you the outfit I have sewn for Mr. Jack," she said to Barnaby

"Oh boy," said Barnaby.

"You don't like it?"

"No, I love it. I was just thinking about what my mother will say when she sees her afghan on Felton Jack's back."

"She will be overjoyed."

The back seat of the limo was cavernous. "Does this TV work?" Barnaby asked the driver.

"Yes, sir. One hundred and seventy-eight channels. It's a satellite."

Barnaby switched it on and he and Babette watched a "Melrose Place" rerun on the way to the airport. It was the one where Kimberly tries to burn down the apartment complex.

They arrived at Kennedy Airport and there he was, Felton Jack, standing outside the baggage claim, looking lost.

"Felton Jack?" asked the driver.

"Yes, that's me."

"Hop in, sir."

And he did, squeezing between Babette and Barnaby on the back seat.

"Thank you for coming on such short notice, Mr. Jack," said Barnaby.

"That's Sir Jack. *Sir Jack.* I was knighted you know."

"Why?" asked Babette.

"Well, er, uh, gallant deeds! Like any other knight!" said Felton.

"Oh, of course!" said Barnaby. "Sir Jack, I'd like to introduce you to Babette."

"Yes, yesss. Babette. We have met before, haven't we?"

"Yes, Sir Jack, backstage at the Grandson concert. You were eating sandwiches . . ."

"Was I? Sandwiches? What kind?"

"I believe they were salami sandwiches," said Babette.

"Oh! Salami. Salami, salami, salami. I do love salami. With a passion!"

"Bridget actually told me you requested bologna to eat backstage this evening," said Barnaby.

"Did I? Bologna? Well, yes, that makes sense, because I adore bologna, too. Bologna, bologna, bologna. Mm-mmm! Scrumptious!"

"Sir Jack," interrupted Babette, "In addition to being your biggest fan, I am also an aspiring clothing designer."

"Are you? Then you should meet my dear friend Kiki . . . oh my . . . I am sorry . . . dear, dear Kiki. How many times did I tell him. 'Look before you step in an elevator! Because doors open for no reason!' They do! And they did."

"It was tragic," said Barnaby.

"It was terrible," offered Babette. "But I hope you will like the outfit I made for you. Mr. Krayola was a big inspiration to the design."

"Well let me have a look-see then."

Babette removed the afghan jumpsuit from the box. Felton Jack put his hands to his mouth.

"Do you hate it?" asked Babette.

"Hate it? Hate it? My dear, I adore it. It's as if Kiki himself created it! I think it will fit perfectly! Thank you my children, thank you. Now, driver, drive faster! We have a concert to put on!"

QUICK SUMMARY OF CHAPTER 6

★ Barnaby was in big trouble because he owed Beauregard Bumblebee tuna, and he couldn't pay up.

★ Beauregard had two of his goons threaten Barnaby, to make him pay up.

★ Barnaby asked Bridget if Felton Jack could fly into town and play a benefit concert for him. Bridget said "No problem."

★ Barnaby got Babette to help him.

★ Babette learned how to use question-and-answer flashcards to help her remember important things about the concert.

★ Barnaby helped Babette by reading the question-and-answer flashcard questions aloud.

★ She then went on a radio program to promote the Bumblebee Benefit Concert.

★ Barnaby made posters to promote the concert.

★ You can make study posters to help you remember important information for tests and quizzes.

★ Babette had to make Felton Jack an outfit for the show.

★ She tried to sew an outfit without following directions. It was too small.

★ She learned how to read directions, and the next outfit was much better.

★ If you are having trouble reading directions or studying, never be afraid to ask for help. That is what your teachers are there for. Your parents and friends can help a lot, too.

★When you sit down to study, you have to get rid of all distractions—anything that will take you away from your studying.

★Barnaby and Babette picked up Sir Felton Jack at the airport. He loved the outfit Babette had created, and looked forward to the concert.

Chapter 7
Test-Taking Strategies

The Mellman Middle School gym was rocking, packed to the rafters with middle schoolers and their parents, all there to hear their favorite Felton Jack songs. The posters and Babette's appearance on the "Raging Randy" show had done the trick—the Felton Jack Bumblebee Benefit Concert was the place to be in New York that Friday night.

Backstage, Felton Jack ate one bologna sandwich after another.

"B-b-bologna bologna b-b-bologna" he stuttered between bites.

Barnaby stood next to a pile of Bumbleebee tuna cans packed in oil, beaming. He prepared to introduce the pop star and looked around for Babette. She was gone. He yelled into the girls' locker room.

"Babette! Concert time!"

"I cannot do it," she called back. Barnaby went in. "Get out!" she screamed. "This is the girl's locker room!"

"What's the matter?" asked Barnaby.

"I feel like I feel before I am about to take a test," explained Babette. "I cannot do it, I can't remember the lines to my songs, it is all just too much. My brain is frozen. My stomach is in knots."

"Well, let's go through your preparation."

"Okay."

"Did you get a good night's sleep last night?"

"Yes."

"Have you eaten a good meal today?"

"Yes."

"Have you had enough time to relax and think about what you need to do? You aren't feeling rushed?"

"No, no. I have been here for close to an hour now. There has been plenty of time to relax."

"Have you reviewed the songs you need to sing?"

"Yes, yes."

"Would reviewing them with me help?"

"I suppose."

So they sang "Bad Alligator" together.

"Now if you forget the lyrics on stage, what do you do?"

"Panic?"

"No," replied Barnaby. "You mouth the word 'watermelon'—an old trick I learned in children's choir. Then you can just say the microphone was faulty."

"Thank you, Barnaby. I feel much better."

Preparing for a Test Tip

The things Babette is doing to relax for the concert are things you can do to relax before a test. Again, they are the following:

★ Get enough sleep

★ Eat a good meal

★ Review the material alone or with a friend

★ Don't rush—give yourself enough time to relax in the classroom before the exam begins

★ Don't panic—take long deep breaths, pulling air in through your nose and exhaling through your mouth.

In addition to these relaxation techniques, there are specific things you can do once you are taking a test that can help you.

★ Read the directions carefully. We talked about this earlier. Make sure you know exactly what is expected of you. Sometimes a teacher asks you to write essays on two out of three topics she provides. If you don't read the directions, you could waste valuable time writing essays for all three topics.

★ Answer the questions you know first. If you don't know the first question, go to the second. If you don't know that one, go to the third. Just answer one you know first, then go back and hit the hard ones.

★ Don't watch everyone else. Some people fly through tests. They write fast, they finish early, they look like they know everything. Sometimes they do. Sometimes, they're just careless and rush needlessly though the test. Don't worry about other people. Worry about yourself.

★ Spend more time on the questions that count more. If a question is worth ten points, don't spend half the class answering it. If a question is worth fifty points, you can devote a lot of time answering it.

★ Don't second-guess yourself. Unless you know for sure that you answered a question wrong, don't go back and change an answer. Trust yourself. It's hard, but it's usually the best way.

"Are you ready to rock?" asked Barnaby.

"I am ready to rock," replied Babette.

And she did. It was the best concert of Felton Jack's career, and, of course, he looked better than he had in quite some time.

QUICK SUMMARY OF CHAPTER 7

★ Mellman Middle School was packed to the rafters with Felton Jack fans.

★ Babette got nervous before the concert. Barnaby led her through some relaxation techniques. There are also relaxation techniques you can use for a test at school.

★ The concert was a smashing success.

Chapter 8
The End

"Here's your tuna, Beauregard," said Barnaby. "A life-time supply of Bumblebee tuna, packed in oil."

"Thank you, Barnaby," said Beauregard. "I knew I could count on you."

"Meow," said Brenda.

"Can I ask you a question, Beauregard?" asked Barnaby.

"Shoot, kid."

"Why did you get so angry over the tuna and have your goons threaten me?"

"Being a talking cat gets frustrating. Especially when your girlfriend doesn't speak at all."

"Girlfriend?"

"Yes, I suppose you could say Brenda is my girlfriend. And, well, I haven't been able to get close to her because she doesn't speak."

"I see. So tuna is the only thing you two have in common!"

"Exactly, Barnaby, my boy. You *are* a supergenius."

"So, when there is no tuna . . ." continued Barnaby.

"There is no Barnaby and Brenda in love!"

"Fascinating."

"Yes, I'm sorry, Barnaby. Love makes you do dumb things sometimes. It will never happen again. Now, please, if you will excuse us. Brenda?"

"Meow?" said Brenda.

"Let's eat!"

"Meow!" said Brenda.

"That Beauregard," chuckled Barnaby. "Hey, Babette, listen. I'm sorry we got a little off-track with improving your study habits. Things just went haywire."

"*Au contraire,*" replied Babette. "The things I have learned helping Grandpa Gus and putting together the Felton Jack concert taught me just as much as Beauregard's *Of Mice and Men* note-taking tips and Bridget's schedule-making advice. I learned how to follow directions, how to memorize, and how to practice relaxation techniques before an exam."

"Good, I'm glad."

"Plus, I was able to design an outfit for Sir Felton Jack and secure a promise from him."

"Really?" replied Barnaby. "And that promise is what?"

"Sir Felton Jack promised that if I get good grades and get into Fashion High and get good grades there and get into Fashion College and get good grades there, he will give me the chance to replace Kiki Krayola as his personal fashion designer!"

"Wonderful!" exclaimed Barnaby.

"Yes, it is. So goodbye, Barnaby. It has been a wonderful day. But now I must go study for my test on *Of Mice and Men*, and for so many other things if I ever want to see my goals come true."

"See you Monday at school."

"*Au revoir,* Barnaby. Until Monday."

Quick Quiz Answers

QUICK QUIZ 1 ANSWERS

Name: Bridget		Date: Wednesday
Time of Day		
6 a.m.	Get up, have breakfast	
7 a.m.	Wake Ihop for Yoga class	
8 a.m.	Wake Thack and Sailor	
9 a.m.		
10 a.m.	"Regis and Kathie Lee" (Thack)	
11 a.m.	Tambourine lesson (Sailor)	
noon	Tutoring (Ihop and Sailor)	
1 p.m.	Serve protein-enriched health shakes (all 3)	
2 p.m.	Pick up uniforms at dry cleaners	
3 p.m.	School (Ihop), Eye doctor (Sailor), Drum lesson (Thack)	
4 p.m.	Naptime (all 3), Yoga for Bridget	
5 p.m.	Chiropractor – (Bridget and Ihop)	
6 p.m.	Intvw: "MTV Style" (Thack and Sailor)	
7 p.m.	Soundcheck – London Children's Hospital	
8 p.m.	Concert – London Children's Hospital	
9 p.m.	Speed away in limousine	
10 p.m.	Bedtime – (all 3)	
11 p.m.		
midnight		

QUICK QUIZ 2 ANSWERS

Dates: Sept. 2 – Sept. 6			Personal Schedule of Bridget		
Time of Day	**Monday**	**Tuesday**	**Wednesday**	**Thursday**	**Friday**
6 a.m.					
7 a.m.	wake up lhop for yoga	wake up lhop for yoga	wake up lhop for yoga	wake up lhop for yoga	wake up lhop for yoga
8 a.m.	wake Thack and Sailor	wake Thack and Sailor	wake Thack and Sailor	wake Thack and Sailor	wake Thack and Sailor
9 a.m.	breakfast w/parents – Serve protein-enriched shakes	breakfast w/parents – Serve protein-enriched shakes	breakfast w/parents – Serve protein-enriched shakes	breakfast w/parents – Serve protein-enriched shakes	breakfast w/parents – Serve protein-enriched shakes
10 a.m.					
11 a.m.					
12 p.m.	home schooling for band	home schooling for band	home schooling for band	home schooling for band	home schooling for band
1 p.m.	Serve protein-enriched health shakes	Serve protein-enriched health shakes	Serve protein-enriched health shakes	Serve protein-enriched health shakes	Serve protein-enriched health shakes
2 p.m.					
3 p.m.	Thack drum lesson Sailor tambourine lesson	Thack drum lesson Sailor tambourine lesson	Thack drum lesson Sailor tambourine lesson	Thack drum lesson Sailor tambourine lesson	Thack drum lesson Sailor tambourine lesson
4 p.m.	naptime for Thack and Sailor	naptime for Thack and Sailor	naptime for Thack and Sailor	naptime for Thack and Sailor	naptime for Thack and Sailor
5 p.m.	make goo-goo eyes at lhop	make goo-goo eyes at lhop	make goo-goo eyes at lhop	make goo-goo eyes at lhop	make goo-goo eyes at lhop
6 p.m.					
7 p.m.					
8 p.m.	Serve protein-enriched health shakes	Serve protein-enriched health shakes	Serve protein-enriched health shakes	Serve protein-enriched health shakes	Serve protein-enriched health shakes

Quick Quiz 3 Answers

Dates: Week One			Personal Schedule of _Babette_		
Time of Day	**Monday**	**Tuesday**	**Wednesday**	**Thursday**	**Friday**
6 a.m.					
7 a.m.					
8 a.m.	Homeroom	Homeroom	Homeroom	Homeroom	Homeroom
9 a.m.	English	Band	English	Band	English
10 a.m.	Math	Math	Math	Math	Math
11 a.m.	Gym	Lunch	Gym	Lunch	Gym
12 p.m.	Lunch	Social Studies	Lunch	Social Studies	Lunch
1 p.m.	Science	Science	Science	Science	Science
2 p.m.	Social Studies	Study Hall	Social Studies	Study Hall	Social Studies
3 p.m.					
4 p.m.					
5 p.m.					
6 p.m.					
7 p.m.					
8 p.m.					

Quick Quiz 4 Answers

Dates: Week One			Personal Schedule of Babette		
Time of Day	**Monday**	**Tuesday**	**Wednesday**	**Thursday**	**Friday**
6 a.m.					
7 a.m.					
8 a.m.	Homeroom	Homeroom	Homeroom	Homeroom	Homeroom
9 a.m.	English **read through ch.2**	Band	English	Band	English **Quiz through Ch.3**
10 a.m.	Math	Math	Math **Ex 1.1 & 1.2 Due**	Math	Math **read through p.25**
11 a.m.	Gym	Lunch	Gym	Lunch	Gym **10 pull-ups**
12 p.m.	Lunch	Social Studies **read section 1.3**	Lunch	Social Studies	Lunch
1 p.m.	Science	Science	Science	Science **Lab Report Due**	Science
2 p.m.	Social Studies	Study Hall	Social Studies	Study Hall	Social Studies **read section 1.4**
3 p.m.					
4 p.m.					
5 p.m.					
6 p.m.					
7 p.m.					
8 p.m.					

QUICK QUIZ 5 ANSWERS

Revise Babette's Notes

Here are Beauregard's revised notes on *Of Mice and Men*.

Lennie and George
Are friends
George: little and smart
George: their leader
Lennie Small: big and dumb
Lennie: likes mice and rabbits. Keeps a mouse in his pocket.
George talks mean to Lennie, but he really loves him.
He just gets frustrated because Lennie is so dumb.
Lennie and George are ranch hands.
A ranch hand does the hard work on a ranch.
They travel from ranch to ranch.

Setting
A stream or lake in the woods and a ranch near the highway.

Plot
Lennie and George got run out of the town of Weed.
Lennie hurt a woman in Weed so they had to run away.
They hid in a ditch so they wouldn't get caught.
They took a bus to a new ranch.
They stopped at a lake in the woods to rest for the night.
Lennie had a dead mouse in his pocket that he was petting.
George made him give it to him and George threw it in the woods.

Lenny killed the mouse by accident in his pocket by petting it too rough. Lennie is big and the mouse is small.

George told Lennie to get firewood and Lennie got the mouse back instead.
George threw it even farther into the woods.
George told Lennie the story of what they'll do when the get their stake.
(A stake is a good amount of money.)
Lennie told the story about buying some land and raising animals, especially rabbits.
They went to sleep.

QUICK QUIZ 6 ANSWERS

The Prisoners' News

Who
Grandson Does Good Time

When
Grandson's August 23 Concert at Liverpool Prison

Where

What*
author
opinion

Yesterday's Grandson concert was the <u>hottest show</u> to hit the British Prison System since The Rolling Stones played the Thames Correctional Facility in 1979. I was there for that show, serving five to ten years for stealing Q-Tips from the London Hospital for the Ear, and I was at Liverpool Prison for last night's Grandson show.

What
(<u>I'm currently serving a life sentence for calling Prince Charles "Prince Curlicue."</u>)

by Inmate #45J6732F

The crowd was in high spirits as Grandson took the stage. Such fine looking young lads. <u>Sailor</u> won us over immediately when he asked, "How many of you think I'm pretty?" From there, Grandson launched into their international number one smash hit "Good Guy Groove." Those boys sure were good players.

Who

What*
author
opinion
<u>Ihop's guitar crackled like the fire I set in the warden's office. Thackeray's drums burst like rotten tomatoes on a car's windshield. And Sailor's voice was as smooth as my lawyer</u> is when she asks the judge why a nice guy like me, <u>Inmate #45J6732F</u>, has to stay in prison for so long for calling Prince Charles "Prince Curlicue."

Who

I wasn't really paying attention for the rest of the show, but from the sound of the crowd, I <u>bet it was really, really good.</u>

What*
author
opinion

Beauregard's Summary of the Article for Grandpa Grandson

This article was written by an inmate at Liverpool Prison for <u>The Prisoners' News</u>. It is about a concert Grandson **(Who)** gave at <u>Liverpool Prison</u> **(Where)** on <u>August 23rd</u> **(When)**. The inmate liked the concert. It is the best show he has seen since he saw the Rolling Stones in 1973 at another prison. He was serving time for stealing Q-tips then. Now he is serving time for calling Prince Charles "Prince Curlicue." Grandson played their hit song "Good Guy Groove." Grandson are:

1. Ihop—guitar player

2. Thackeray—drummer

3. Sailor—singer **(Who)**

The inmate liked the way they played **(What*/author opinion)**. Grandson reminded him of a bunch of crimes he'd committed **(What*/author opinion)**. The inmate didn't pay much attention to the concert, though.

QUICK QUIZ 7 ANSWERS

ARTICLE 3

Spun Magazine
Supermodels Love Grandson
Who · by <u>Johnny Lightning</u>

When · <u>August 25</u>, Silver Dollar Arcade
Melbourne, Australia

Who · <u>Grandson's</u> surprise concert at the
Where · <u>Silver Dollar Arcade</u> wasn't a surprise to the world's
Who · <u>supermodels</u>. Nobody, except for writers like me, was supposed to know that Grandson was playing a surprise show at this tiny video game arcade in Melbourne, Australia. Somehow, word got out, and before you knew it the Silver Dollar Arcade was transformed from a room full of kids and video games into a room
Who · full of <u>supermodels and Arab sheiks.</u>

Who · Supermodel <u>Claudia Shiftless</u>
Who · arrived on the arm of <u>Sheik</u>
Who · <u>Magic Salami</u>; supermodel <u>Tyra Tanks</u> arrived on the arm of <u>Sheik</u>
Who · <u>Vava Voom</u>; and supermodel <u>Courtney Dove</u> arrived on the arm · Who of <u>Sheik I. Kiltcurt</u>. · Who

With all of the sheiks and supermodels, it was hard for me to focus on Grandson, who played <u>their hit song "Good Guy Groove"</u> · What quietly in the corner. I did notice that <u>Sailor Grandson</u> was more · Who interested in the Mortal Kombat video game over by the wall than he was in singing, but Grandson sounded just fine, anyway.

After the show, I played against Sailor in Mortal Kombat, and he beat me in front of all those supermodels. They laughed at me for losing to a teenager. <u>It was</u> · What* <u>embarrassing.</u> · author opinion

Babettes's Summary of the Article for Grandpa Gus

This article is about a concert <u>Grandson</u> (**Who**) played on <u>August 25</u> (**When**) at the <u>Silver Dollar Arcade</u> (**Where**) in <u>Melbourne, Australia</u> (**Where**). It was written by <u>Johnny Lightning</u> (**Who**). <u>He liked the show</u> (**What*, author opinion**), but he was more interested in all of the <u>supermodels</u> (**Who**) that showed up with rich <u>Arab sheiks</u> (**Who**). He mentioned <u>three couples</u> (**Who**):

1. Claudia Shiftless and Sheik Magic Salami

2. Tyra Tanks and Sheik Vava Voom

3. Courtney Dove and Sheik I. Kiltcurt

After the concert, the writer played Sailor in a game of Mortal Kombat and lost. <u>He was embarrassed</u> (**What*, author opinion**).

Quick Quiz 8 Answers

1. B (Article 1)
2. A (Article 3)
3. C (Article 2)
4. A (Article 3)
5. C (Article 3)
6. A (Articles 1 and 2)
7. B (Articles 1, 2, and 3)
8. C (Article 1)
9. B (Articles 1, 2 and 3)
10. C (Background story)

QUICK QUIZ 9 ANSWERS

Barnaby's Actual Schedule

Name: Barnaby	Date:

Time of Day	
6 a.m.	
7 a.m.	
8 a.m.	Prepare Babette for the "Raging Randy" show
9 a.m.	Make posters
10 a.m.	Tape posters all over town
11 a.m.	↓ ↓ ↓
noon	Buy lots of bologna, white bread, and mustard
1 p.m.	↓ ↓ ↓ ↓
2 p.m.	Put up the stage in the gym
3 p.m.	Assemble the school band for song practice
4 p.m.	↓ ↓ ↓ ↓
5 p.m.	Pick up Felton Jack at the airport
6 p.m.	Bumblebee Benefit Concert
7 p.m.	↓ ↓ ↓
8 p.m.	Go to A&P and buy Bumblebee tuna before store closes
9 p.m.	
10 p.m.	
11 p.m.	
midnight	

Babette's Actual Schedule

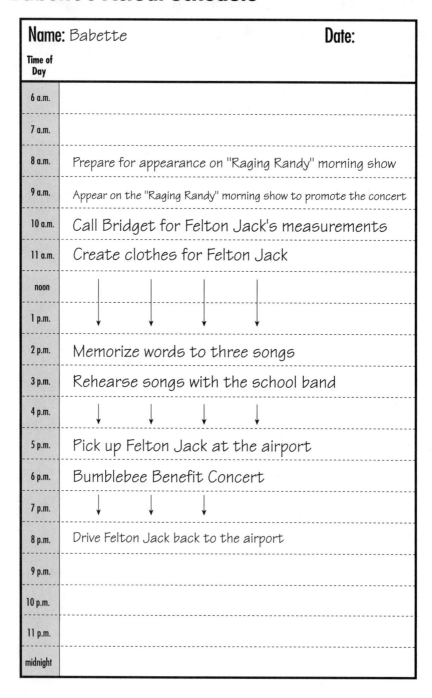

Name: Babette	Date:
Time of Day	
6 a.m.	
7 a.m.	
8 a.m.	Prepare for appearance on "Raging Randy" morning show
9 a.m.	Appear on the "Raging Randy" morning show to promote the concert
10 a.m.	Call Bridget for Felton Jack's measurements
11 a.m.	Create clothes for Felton Jack
noon	
1 p.m.	
2 p.m.	Memorize words to three songs
3 p.m.	Rehearse songs with the school band
4 p.m.	
5 p.m.	Pick up Felton Jack at the airport
6 p.m.	Bumblebee Benefit Concert
7 p.m.	
8 p.m.	Drive Felton Jack back to the airport
9 p.m.	
10 p.m.	
11 p.m.	
midnight	

FLASHCARD QUICK QUIZ 10 ANSWERS

1.

Front

Q: What hit songs will Felton Jack be singing?

Back

A: 1. "Bad Alligator"

2. "Rocket Rock"

3. "Sharon's Song"

2.

Front

Q: When will the concert start?

Back

A: 6 p.m.

3.

Front

| Q: Where is the concert? |

Back

| A: Mellman Middle School Gymnasium |

4.

Front

Q: What is the price of admission?

Back

A: One can of Bumblebee tuna packed in oil, NOT water.

APPENDIX: STUDY AIDS

DAILY PLANNER PAGE

Name:	Date:
Time of Day	
6 a.m.	
7 a.m.	
8 a.m.	
9 a.m.	
10 a.m.	
11 a.m.	
noon	
1 p.m.	
2 p.m.	
3 p.m.	
4 p.m.	
5 p.m.	
6 p.m.	
7 p.m.	
8 p.m.	
9 p.m.	
10 p.m.	
11 p.m.	
midnight	

WEEKLY PLANNER PAGE

Dates:			Personal Schedule of _____		
Time of Day	**Monday**	**Tuesday**	**Wednesday**	**Thursday**	**Friday**
6 a.m.					
7 a.m.					
8 a.m.					
9 a.m.					
10 a.m.					
11 a.m.					
12 p.m.					
1 p.m.					
2 p.m.					
3 p.m.					
4 p.m.					
5 p.m.					
6 p.m.					
7 p.m.					
8 p.m.					

ABOUT THE AUTHOR

Chris Kensler is a writer and editor from Indiana. He has written articles about college admissions and issues affecting soap opera actors.

NOTES

NOTES

NOTES

NOTES

NOTES

NOTES

NOTES

NOTES

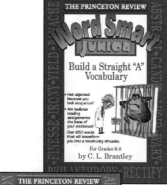
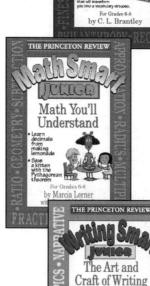

FIND US...

International

Hong Kong
4/F Sun Hung Kai Centre
30 Harbour Road, Wan Chai,
Hong Kong
Tel: (011)85-2-517-3016

Japan
Fuji Building 40, 15-14
Sakuragaokacho, Shibuya Ku,
Tokyo 150, Japan
Tel: (011)81-3-3463-1343

Korea
Tae Young Bldg, 944-24,
Daechi- Dong, Kangnam-Ku
The Princeton Review- ANC
Seoul, Korea 135-280,
South Korea
Tel: (011)82-2-554-7763

Mexico City
PR Mex S De RL De Cv
Guanajuato 228 Col. Roma
06700 Mexico D.F., Mexico
Tel: 525-564-9468

Montreal
666 Sherbrooke St.
West, Suite 202
Montreal, QC H3A 1E7 Canada
Tel: (514) 499-0870

Pakistan
1 Bawa Park - 90 Upper Mall
Lahore, Pakistan
Tel: (011)92-42-571-2315

Spain
Pza. Castilla, 3 - 5° A, 28046
Madrid, Spain
Tel: (011)341-323-4212

Taiwan
155 Chung Hsiao East Road
Section 4 - 4th Floor,
Taipei R.O.C., Taiwan
Tel: (011)886-2-751-1243

Thailand
Building One, 99 Wireless Road
Bangkok, Thailand 10330
Tel: (662) 256-7080

Toronto
1240 Bay Street, Suite 300
Toronto M5R 2A7 Canada
Tel: (800) 495-7737
Tel: (716) 839-4391

Vancouver
4212 University Way NE,
Suite 204
Seattle, WA 98105
Tel: (206) 548-1100

National (U.S.)

We have over 60 offices around the U.S. and
run courses in over 400 sites. For courses and locations
within the U.S. call 1 (800) 2/Review and you will be
routed to the nearest office.